교사들을 위한

# 교실영어와 학교영어

교사들을 위한

# 교실영어와 학교영어

엄철주 · 오경옥 · 오희진 · 김희화 공저

전남대학교출판부

# 머리말

지구촌 시대의 도래와 함께 오늘날 우리는 영어의 홍수 속에서 살아가고 있다. 넘쳐나는 영어 정보의 소비자와 생산자로서 우리는 이른바 문화자본의 중요한 일부가 되어버린 영어를 얻기 위해 분주하다. 영어 교육의 주 무대인 초·중등학교를 비롯한 일선 교육현장에서도 학생들의 의사소통능력을 기르기 위한 다양한 변화가 관찰되고 있다. 이중에서도 교사들의 영어구사능력을 강화하는 연수를 확대하여 영어를 통한 영어수업(Teaching English through English) 능력을 제고하고 있는 점은 주목할 만하다.

사실 영어를 사용하여 영어를 가르친다는 것은 매우 당연한 일이지만 현실은 그렇지 못하였다. 하지만 이제는 각급 학교에서 국제 교류가 활발히 진행되고, 해외 장기체류경험이 있는 학생들이 증가하고 있으며, 학교 안팎에서 구어능력의 중요성을 점차 강조하고 있어서 영어를 통한 영어 수업은 교사들에게는 필수 과제가 되고 있다.

이런 점에서 볼 때, 학교 현장에서 교사들이 수업이나 학내행사를 진행하면서 사용할 수 있는 다양한 영어 표현을 다루고 있는 이 책은 영어 활용수업에 관심이 있거나 국제교류 업무를 담당하고 있는 선생님들에게 실제적으로 상당한 도움이 되리라 생각한다. 이 책은 크게 교실영어와 학교영어 두 부분으로 나뉘어 있는데, 교실영어는 수업을 시작하여 끝을 맺을 때까지 수업의 전 과정에서 활용되는 표현들을 Pattern Practice와 Useful Expression을 중심으로 폭넓게 다루고 있다. 또한 학교영어는 학내의 주요 행사를 진행하거나 생활지도를 하면서 필요한 영어 표현들을 우리말과 함께 다양하게 소개하여 관련 상황에서 손쉽게 활용할 수 있도록 하였다.

아무쪼록 이 작은 책자가 일선 교단에서 영어교육에 힘을 쏟고 있는 선생님들이나 예비교사들에게 조금이나마 보탬이 될 수 있기를 바란다.

2008년 12월

저자 씀

# 목차

## Part I 교실 영어
*Classroom English*

## Part Ⅱ 학교 영어
*School English*

# Part I

# 교실 영어

## *Classroom English*

# 1. 수업 시작 (Beginning of the Lesson)

## 1) 도입 (Introduction)

### (1) 인사하기 (Greetings)

교사가 처음 교실에 들어가서 전체 학생들에게 인사하고 새 학기 첫 날 자신을 소개하는 표현으로, 학생들의 안부나 그 날의 날씨, 학생 개개인의 기분과 건강 상태 등에 관하여 짧은 대화를 나눈다.

#### Dialogue Practice ①

T: Good afternoon, everybody.

Ss: Good afternoon, Miss Oh.

T: Well, how's everything, today?

Ss: Pretty good, thank you. How are you?

T: Very well, thank you. And how are you feeling today?

S: I'm well, thank you, Miss Oh.

T: I hope you all had a nice weekend.

#### Dialogue Practice ②

T: Good morning.

Ss: Good morning.

T: How are you?

Ss: Very well, thank you.

T: Did anyone travel anywhere over the weekend?

S: Yes, I went to my father's hometown.

T: Oh, did you? What was the journey like?

S: It was very exciting to walk on the country roads.

T: Good. What else did you do over the weekend? Yes, Ji-Sun?

S: I went to a party.

T: What was it like? Did you enjoy it?

S: Yes. We listened to good music and played games.

T: Good. Have you done your homework?

Ss: Yes.

T: OK, can you collect it, Hee-Young, while I take the role?

>>> '주말에'를 미국식 영어에서는 over the weekend라고 표현하고 영국식 영어에서는 at the weekend라고 표현합니다.

## Pattern Practice

### A. 인사하기 (Greetings)

**1**

| | | |
|---|---|---|
| Good | morning,<br>afternoon,<br>evening, | everybody.<br>Class 2.<br>girls.<br>girls and boys.<br>children.<br>Mr./Mrs./Miss Kim. |

**2**

| | |
|---|---|
| Are you all well<br>How are you<br>How are you feeling | today?<br>this evening? |
| How is it going?<br>How is everything?<br>How are things with you?<br>How have you been doing?<br>How is everyone doing today? | |

| 3 | | |
|---|---|---|
| I hope | you are all feeling | well.<br>fit today. |
| | you all had a nice/good weekend/holiday. | |

| 4 | |
|---|---|
| Fine, thanks, | and you?<br>how about you? |
| Very well,<br>(I'm) not too bad, | thank you.<br>thanks. |

## Useful Expressions

| | |
|---|---|
| 첫인사하기 | ■ How are you (feeling) today?<br>■ How is it going?<br>■ How's everything?<br>■ How's everyone (doing) today?<br>■ How are things with you?<br>■ How have you been doing? |
| 날씨에 대해 대화하기 | ■ Beautiful morning, isn't it?<br>■ Nice day, isn't it? Good day for outdoor activities.<br>■ Good morning. The weather is really wonderful. I want to go outside and sunbathe.<br>■ What a lovely morning! Spring is around the corner.<br>■ Hello, everybody. The weather is getting hotter and hotter. When it is this hot, you'll become easily tired. Get enough rest, so you can stay awake during the classes.<br>■ How are you? Is the weather bothering you? A wise proverb says, "What cannot be cured must be endured." Stay healthy through regular exercise and eat a balanced diet.<br>■ How are you doing? The Monsoon season is with us, so it is quite sticky and irritating. Make sure you carry your umbrellas and stay dry. Please take extra care not to get food poisoning.<br>■ Good morning, everyone. It is rather chilly. Fall is almost over. I wish we could have fall all year round.<br>■ Good morning! There's frost on the ground this morning. Winter is just around the corner. |

| | |
|---|---|
| 개별 학생의 안부 묻기 | ■ You look down today. Is anything wrong?<br>■ How are you today? You look tired. You must have been studying a lot for the mid-term exams. Remember to get some sleep, too!<br>■ How are you feeling today? Your cheek looks swollen. Do you have a toothache? You'd better go to the dentist, before it gets too serious.<br>■ You are late. Where have you been? Why are you limping? Are you hurt? Let me take a look at your ankle. I think you got a bruise.<br>■ I hope you've recovered from your cold. Are you still taking your medication?<br>■ Good. I am glad you have recovered from your cold. How are you feeling now?<br>■ Good morning, Min-Kyeong. How are you doing? What's the matter with your eye? You have to put a patch over your eye. Is your eye infected? |
| 수업시작 유도하기 | ■ Are you ready for this class? Wake up, guys. We have a lot to cover today.<br>■ It's a beautiful morning, isn't it? Today is a perfect day for an outdoor class. Why don't we go out and have class on the benches? Please walk quietly while going out and button your lips. I don't want to disturb the other classes. |

## B. 자기 소개하기 (Introducing yourself)

**5**

| | | |
|---|---|---|
| I'll just | introduce myself.<br>tell you a bit about myself. | My name is ______, spelt_______ |

**6**

| | |
|---|---|
| I | come from ___________.<br>live in ___________.<br>have been working in (for) __________. |

**7**

| | |
|---|---|
| And what about you? | |
| Can you introduce | yourself?<br>your neighbor to me? |

## Useful Expressions

| | |
|---|---|
| 교사 자기소개하기 | ■ I'll be teaching you English this year. I'm happy to have you as my students.<br>■ My name is Mr. Park and I'm your new English teacher.<br>■ I'm a teacher trainee and I'll be teaching you today, tomorrow and Wednesday.<br>■ You will have four lessons with me.<br>■ Let me introduce myself. I am Kim Hyo-Jin. Nice to meet you. |

## (2) 가벼운 대화하기 (Small Talk)

학생들과의 rapport 형성을 위하여 수업 시작 전 학생들이 좋아하는 과목, 교사 등의 학교생활과 주말 계획, 취미 활동, 가족사항 등의 개인 사생활 등에 대하여 짧은 대화를 나누면서 수업 분위기를 조성한다.

## Dialogue Practice ①

T: Which subject do you like most? Do you like English?

S: No, Ms. Kim. I have no interest in any language at all. Instead, I like math. I think math is good for developing logical thinking.

T: That sounds good. But many students think math is their weak point.

S: I like to work out hard math problems. Sometimes, it can take me hours and hours, but when I finish solving them, I feel a really great sense of accomplishment.

T: Excellent! I can imagine how you feel. I was not good at math, so I gave up being a doctor. Keep up the good work, Hyeon-Soo.

S: Thank you, Teacher.

## Dialogue Practice ②

T: Did everyone have a great weekend?

Ss: Yes... No...

T: Mmm... How was your weekend, Gyeong-Jin?

S: Terrible. I had to take care of my little sister instead of going to Se-Mi's birthday party. My parents were very busy, and there was no one else to look after my sister.

T: I'm sorry to hear that but what a good daughter you are!

## A. 주말에 한 일에 대하여 (Small talk about the weekend)

### Pattern Practice

**1**

| Well, | did you have a good<br>did you enjoy the<br>did anyone do anything interesting during the | weekend?<br>holiday? |
|---|---|---|

**2**

| What did you do<br>Can you tell me what you did<br>Did anyone do something special | last night?<br>yesterday after school?<br>over the weekend?<br>during the holidays? |
|---|---|

**3**

| Can<br>Could | you tell us | more about that? | | |
|---|---|---|---|---|
| | | what the | picnic<br>party<br>soccer game | was like? |

**4**

| Oh, you've got a new | shirt<br>dress | on. | It's very nice.<br>It looks good on you. |
|---|---|---|---|
| | hair style. | | |

## Useful Expressions

<table>
<tr><td>주말에 한 일 묻기</td><td>

- I hope you all have had a nice weekend.
- What's new? Do you have any interesting plans for the weekend?
- I hope you enjoyed a nice weekend. If it hadn't rained, it would have been wonderful for a picnic.
- I hope you all have had a nice weekend. Did anyone do something special on the weekend?
- I hope you had a nice weekend. Saturday was a good day to go outside. Did you take advantage of the weather? It was too beautiful of a day to stay at home, so I went out for a drive in the countryside.

</td></tr>
</table>

## B. 학교생활에 대하여 (Small talk about school life)

## Pattern Practice

5

<table>
<tr><td rowspan="2">How do you like<br>How do you feel about</td><td>your new</td><td>school?<br>class?<br>homeroom teacher?<br>friend?</td></tr>
<tr><td colspan="2">a co-ed school?<br>a girls-only school?<br>an after-school program?<br>club activity?</td></tr>
<tr><td>What do you think of</td><td colspan="2">eating in the school cafeteria?<br>making a friend of the opposite gender?</td></tr>
</table>

6

<table>
<tr><td>Why</td><td>are you interested in<br>do you like</td><td rowspan="3">music?</td></tr>
<tr><td>How come</td><td rowspan="2">you don't like<br>you hate</td></tr>
<tr><td>Why is it that</td></tr>
</table>

## Useful Expressions

| | |
|---|---|
| 좋아하는 과목에 대해 묻기 | ▪ What is your favorite subject?<br>▪ Do you like math?<br>▪ Are you interested in music?<br>▪ How come you don't like P. E. class?<br>▪ Can you tell me your favorite subjects?<br>▪ How long have you been studying English?<br>▪ Have you studied English conversation before? |
| 친구에 대해 묻기 | ▪ Who is your closest friend?<br>▪ How many friends do you have?<br>▪ Do you like your partner?<br>▪ Do you have a boy/girl friend?<br>▪ What do you think about friends of the opposite gender?<br>▪ Are you still friends with anyone from your elementary or middle school? |
| 교사에 대해 묻기 | ▪ Who is your homeroom teacher?<br>▪ Do you have any teacher in mind?<br>▪ Do you have any teacher that you admire?<br>▪ Who was your homeroom teacher last year?<br>▪ Who was your favorite teacher in your former school? |
| 시험, 성적에 대해 묻기 | ▪ Did you get good marks on the last exam?<br>▪ Do you cram for exams? Does it work?<br>▪ Do you ever suffer from test anxiety?<br>▪ Have you ever cheated on an exam?<br>▪ Have you ever gotten a scholarship?<br>▪ What do you do to prepare for the university entrance exam?<br>▪ What is the hardest subject you have been studying recently? |
| 기타 학교생활에 대해 묻기 | ▪ What grade are you in?<br>▪ How do you get to school?<br>▪ Which club do you belong to?<br>▪ Where do you go after school?<br>▪ Is your home near or far from school?<br>▪ How long does it take to come to school?<br>▪ Can you name one good thing about this school?<br>▪ What are the inconveniences of attending a co-ed school?<br>▪ Were you happy when you heard you would come to this school? |

## C. 취미에 대하여 (Small talk about hobbies)

### Pattern Practice

**7**

| | | |
|---|---|---|
| What do you do<br>What do you like to do | in | your free time?<br>your spare time? |
| How do you spend | | |

**8**

| | | |
|---|---|---|
| What kind of | music<br>sports<br>books<br>movies | do you like most? |

### Useful Expressions

| | |
|---|---|
| 취미 묻기 | ■ Do you have any hobbies?<br>■ What do you do to relax?<br>■ What are your hobbies?<br>■ Do you like cartoons? Why?<br>■ Which do you like better, being indoors or outdoors? Why?<br>■ Do you belong to any club or organization? |
| 운동에 관한 취미활동 묻기 | ■ What sports do you like?<br>■ Do you like to watch or play?<br>■ Do you like hiking?<br>■ Are you good at soccer?<br>■ Who's your favorite basketball player?<br>■ How long have you been learning (taking) Taekwondo?<br>■ Have you ever gone skiing? Where did you go? |
| 컴퓨터에 관한 취미활동 묻기 | ■ How much TV do you watch a day?<br>■ What's your favorite computer game?<br>■ How often do you go to a video game room?<br>■ How many hours do you work on the computer?<br>■ Playing video games longer than an hour can cause eye trouble. |

| | |
|---|---|
| 기타 취미 활동에 관하여 묻기 | ■ Do you like to dance?<br>■ Are you a good dancer?<br>■ Can you play any musical instruments?<br>■ How long have you been playing the piano?<br>■ Do you like traveling?<br>■ Which country do you want to visit?<br>■ Do you like cooking? Can you cook Ramyeon?<br>■ What's the best book you have ever read?<br>■ What's your favorite TV program? |

## D. 개인 생활에 대하여 (Small talk about personal life)

### Pattern Practice

9

| | | |
|---|---|---|
| Who | is your favorite | singer?<br>actor or actress? |
| What | | subject?<br>movie?<br>Chinese food?<br>English pop song? |

10

| | | |
|---|---|---|
| Do you have | naturally curly hair?<br>the latest Beyonce's album?<br>a personal computer at home? | |
| | any | pets?<br>American friends?<br>brothers or sisters?<br>favorite food in the school cafeteria? |

## Useful Expressions

| | |
|---|---|
| 개인 생활에 대해서 묻기 | ■ When is your birthday?<br>■ What is your date of birth?<br>■ Are you the oldest child in your family?<br>■ What do you want to be?<br>■ What do you want to do when you leave school?<br>■ What do you want to major in when you go to college?<br>■ What does your father want you to be?<br>■ Is there any gap between what you want to be and what your parents want you to be?<br>■ What are you doing to make your dreams come true?<br>■ What do you remember most about your childhood?<br>■ What do you like most about yourself? Least?<br>■ Is there anyone you admire a lot? Who?<br>■ Are you a trusting person?<br>■ Do you like to try new things?<br>■ Are you a pessimist or an optimist?<br>■ Are you a morning person or a night person?<br>■ Are you a vegetarian? |
| 가족에 대해서 묻기 | ■ How large is your family?<br>■ How many are there in your family?<br>■ Does your mother work?<br>■ What does your father do? Is he a public servant?<br>■ What does your sister do? Is she a college student?<br>■ I heard you have a twin brother. Is that right?<br>■ Do you think you are your mother's favorite?<br>■ Who is the black sheep in your family?<br>■ Who has helped you the most in your life?<br>■ What do you think of having a twin brother?<br>■ I heard your older brother attends this school too. What grade is he in? Do I know him?<br>■ Do you feel pressured by your family to behave in a certain way?<br>■ When your parents are at work, do you have to take care of your younger sisters? |

| | |
|---|---|
| 외모에 대해서 묻기 | ■ Who do you think you take after?<br>■ What do you like most about your appearance? Least?<br>■ Have you tried to be on a diet?<br>■ Do you work out to lose weight?<br>■ Did you get your hair permed (cut)?<br>■ That jacket looks good on you. Where did you buy it?<br>■ Do you have any problem sitting in the back? Do you want to move closer to the blackboard/front? |

## 2) 출결 확인하기 (Attendance Check)

### (1) 출석 확인하기 (Checking Attendance)

수업을 시작하기 전에 모든 학생이 출석했는지 점검하고 지각생이나 결석생을 파악하여 그 이유를 확인한다.

#### Dialogue Practice ①

T: Let's see if everyone's here. Are you listening?

S: Yes, Miss Oh.

T: Alright. Su-Yeon.

S: Yes.

T: Su-Min? ... Does anyone know where Su-Min is? Is she absent?

S: I don't know. Perhaps she's ill. She must be in the nurse's room.

T: Yes, she might be. Alright.

#### Dialogue Practice ②

T: Oh, In-Ho! I'm glad you're back. You've missed four lessons!

S: Excuse me? I..

T: You were absent for four lessons last week.

S: Oh yes. I was ill. I had.. er...

T: A cold? Oh, I'm sorry. But you'll catch up, won't you?

S: Yes, of course. Was it Chapter 12?

T: Yes, that's it. Good.

## Pattern Practice

**1**

| Right!<br>Now!<br>OK!<br>Quiet, now, please. | I'm going to<br>I'll<br>Listen while I | call the roll.<br>call your names. |
|---|---|---|
| | Let's see | who's absent.<br>if everyone's here.<br>if you're all here.<br>if anyone's missing/absent. |

**2**

| Is | anybody absent?<br>everybody here? |
|---|---|

**3**

| Who's | absent today?<br>missing?<br>not here? |
|---|---|
| What's | the matter with Jin-Su, today?<br>wrong with Jin-Su today? |
| Has anybody | seen Jin-Su today?<br>any idea where Jin-Su is today? |

**4**

| Where | is Ji-Sun?<br>are In-Ho and Dong-Il? | Sorry, I don't know.<br>Oh, he/she will be here in a minute.<br>He/She called in sick.<br>They're coming. |
|---|---|---|

**5**

<table>
<tr><td rowspan="2">Does anybody know<br>Who knows<br>Can anyone tell me</td><td>where</td><td>Ji-Sun is?<br>In-Ho and Dong-Il are?</td></tr>
<tr><td>when</td><td>Hee-Young will be back?</td></tr>
</table>

**6**

<table>
<tr><td rowspan="3">Ji-Young,</td><td colspan="2">you're back. That's nice/good.</td></tr>
<tr><td rowspan="2">you've</td><td>been absent for 3 days.</td></tr>
<tr><td>missed 6 lessons.</td></tr>
</table>

**7**

| You were | away<br>absent | last week,<br>last Tuesday, | weren't you? |
|---|---|---|---|

*Ans)* (Yes, I was.)

**8**

| What was the matter?<br>Why were you away? | Have you been ill? |
|---|---|

*Ans)* (Well, I had a bad cold.)
(I had an accident.)

**9**

| Oh?<br>Oh dear. | Tell me about it.<br>Sorry to hear that. |
|---|---|

**10**

| Are you<br>Do you feel | better now? |
|---|---|

*Ans)* (Yes, thanks.)

**11**

<table>
<tr><td rowspan="2">You'll have to</td><td>catch up,</td><td>won't you?</td></tr>
<tr><td>ask your friends</td><td>to help you.<br>to tell you what we've done.</td></tr>
</table>

*Ans)* (Yes, alright.)

## Useful Expressions

| | |
|---|---|
| 출석 확인하기 | ■ I'll call your names.<br>■ Is everyone here?<br>■ Now let me call the roll.<br>■ Let's see if everyone is here.<br>■ Let's see if you are all here.<br>■ I'm going to check the register. |
| 결석 학생 묻기 | ■ Who's missing?<br>■ No one is absent?<br>■ Who's absent today?<br>■ Who is not here today?<br>■ Is anybody absent today?<br>■ Let's see who is absent. |
| 결석 이유 묻기<br>* unexcused absence<br>: 사고결<br>* excused absence<br>: 공결<br>* excused absence for being sick<br>: 병결 | ■ Does anyone know where he/she is?<br>■ Do you know why he is absent?<br>■ He called in sick today.<br>※ call in sick: 전화로 병결을 알리다.<br>■ Jinsu is out sick today.<br>■ He wasn't feeling well, so he went home.<br>■ He left early.<br>■ He's got the flu/a cold.<br>■ He is in bed with the flu/a cold.<br>■ I think he/she skipped the class.<br>■ His case is an excused absence.<br>■ He was absent from the third class.<br>■ Sorry, I don't know. / I have no idea. |

>>> 출석을 부를 때 check the register, call the register라는 표현을 쓸 수 있다.

## (2) 지각생 확인하기 (Checking for Tardy)

수업에 늦게 들어온 학생에게 늦은 이유를 묻고 다음부터 수업시간을 잘 지킬 것을 지도한다.

### Dialogue Practice ①

T: Hello, Min-Young. You're a bit late today.

S: Yes, Miss Oh, I'm sorry.

T: Well, where have you been?

S: ...er... I forgot my book and I go...

T: You went back for it?

S: Yes.

T: You shouldn't have gone back for it. You could have borrowed one, or shared. Anyway, Min-Young, sit down now. Let's get on with the lesson.

### Dialogue Practice ②

T: Good afternoon, Ju-Hee, er.. what..?

S: Good afternoon, Miss Oh, I'm sorry I'm late today.

T: What happened? Did you miss the bus or was the traffic heavy today?

S: No... er... actually I started out late.

T: Well, never mind. Please take a seat. And would somebody explain to Ju-Hee what we've done so far?

S: I will.

T: Yes? Go on...

## Pattern Practice

1

| Did you | miss the bus<br>get up late<br>get stuck in traffic<br>set out late | or | forget the time?<br>were you delayed?<br>was the bus late? |
|---|---|---|---|

Ans) (I went to see the doctor.)
(I took the wrong bus.)
(I slept in. = I overslept.)
(I got up late and missed the bus.)
(I forgot to bring my homework and went back home for it.)
(I was called by the teacher because I wasn't wearing a name tag.)
(The traffic was so heavy that I couldn't make it on time.)

2

| Well, | it's okay<br>it doesn't matter | today,<br>just this once,<br>this time, | but next time, try to be on time. |
|---|---|---|---|

3

| Well, | you shouldn't really<br>actually, you shouldn't | have | done that.<br>come so late.<br>been playing.<br>been to the school store. |
|---|---|---|---|

4

| Well, you | ought to<br>should | have | set out earlier.<br>come on time, really.<br>asked someone to tell me.<br>told me before if you had to go to the doctor. |
|---|---|---|---|

5

| Alright, but, | you must not<br>you should not<br>you should try not to<br>could you please try not to | forget (it)<br>be late | again.<br>next time.<br>next lesson. |
|---|---|---|---|

6

| Sit down now please.<br>Would you sit down, please?<br>Go and sit down, then. | Right! Back to<br>Let's get on with<br>Let's get back to<br>Right, we'll go on with | our work.<br>the lesson.<br>what we were doing. |
|---|---|---|

### Useful Expressions

| | |
|---|---|
| 늦은 이유 묻기 | ■ You are late again.<br>■ You are tardy for class.<br>■ Why are you late?<br>■ Where have you been?<br>■ What happened?<br>■ Did you get up late?<br>■ Did you oversleep?<br>■ Did you sleep in?<br>■ Did you stay up all night and wake up late?<br>■ You missed the bus? That doesn't sound like a good excuse.<br>■ It's you again. What's the matter with you? (⇒ rude) |
| 늦지 않도록 경고하기 | ■ We started fifteen minutes ago.<br>■ Don't be late again.<br>■ Try to be on time next time.<br>■ No more excuse. Here's your detention slip. I'll see you after school.<br>■ You need to be here on time. Understand? |

>>> detention slip: 벌로서 방과 후 학교에 남으라는 쪽지

## 3) 교실 정돈하기 (Classroom Arrangement)

### (1) 칠판과 좌석 정리하기 (Cleaning Blackboard and Arranging Desks)

칠판이 잘 닦여져 있고 교탁 및 칠판 주변이 정돈되어 있는지 확인하여 깨끗한 환경에서 공부할 수 있도록 교실을 정리한다.

### Dialogue Practice ①

T: The blackboard is not cleaned.
I can see you had a math class before English.
Who is the duty student?

S: I am on duty this week. I am so sorry. I forgot to clean the board.

T: Your class is usually very clean and tidy, so I will give you a break. But, I hope that this will never happen again. Come up, and clean the board, please.

S: Yes, teacher.

## Dialogue Practice ②

T: Hey, why is this classroom so messy? Didn't you clean it up?

Ss: Yes, we did during the lunch break, sir.

T: You see? It looks as dirty as it did in the morning.

Ss: The arts class finished late today, so we didn't have enough time to put everything back in place.

T: You have alway been good at making excuses. I don't want to see the classroom this dirty, again. Do I make myself clear?

Ss: Yes, sir. We will clean up the classroom right after this class.

T: Now, you know what you have to do.

## Pattern Practice

**1**

| Please | can<br>will | you<br>someone | clean | the blackboard?<br>the whiteboard? |
|---|---|---|---|---|

Ans) (Yes, I will.)
(Me!)

**2**

| Would | you<br>someone | mind | cleaning the board? |
|---|---|---|---|

Ans) (No, I'll do it.)
(Alright.)

**3**

| Just clean<br>Leave<br>Don't clean | this<br>that | half.<br>section.<br>part.<br>bit.<br>side. |
|---|---|---|

| Not<br>Only | this<br>that | bit.<br>section.<br>part. | Thank you. |
|---|---|---|---|

**4**

| Could you clean the | top<br>bottom | left-hand<br>right-hand | corner, please? |
|---|---|---|---|

Ans) (Yes, of course.)
(Certainly, Mr. Kim.)
(This bit, here?)
(Here do you mean?)

**5**

| Please could you erase | words<br>sentences<br>drawings | on the left<br>on the right | at the top?<br>at the bottom? |
|---|---|---|---|

**6**

| Erase | everything<br>it all | please. | Thanks.<br>Thank you. |
|---|---|---|---|
| Leave this on | | | |

## Useful Expressions

| | |
|---|---|
| 칠판 지우기 | ■ Erase everything, please.<br>■ Don't clean this side.<br>■ Would you clean the blackboard/whiteboard?<br>■ Could you clean the bottom right-hand corner?<br>■ Can somebody erase the board?<br>■ Leave the right half of the board as it is. Only erase the left half. I see some students are still writing down the lesson. |
| 칠판 주변 정리하기 | ■ Would you clean the chalkboard?<br>■ Didn't you have enough time after the last class to clean it?<br>■ Would somebody mind cleaning the board? Please do it before the bell rings. I really hate chalk dust. If you breathe in it, it can damage your lungs.<br>■ Could you clean the bottom left-hand corner? No, bottom part. O.K. Thank you. You did a good job.<br>■ Clean everything off, please. Empty the chalk bin at the bottom and clean the ledge, too. |

| 분필, 칠판지우개 관리하기 | ■ We have run out of white chalk.<br>■ Will you go and get some chalk?<br>■ Go and get some chalk from the office.<br>■ Go and see if there's any next door.<br>■ Go and ask Mr. Kim for some pieces of chalk.<br>■ Would you go and look for some chalk for me, please?<br>■ Does anyone know where the chalk is kept?<br>■ Do you know if there's any coloured chalk?<br>■ Can you clean off the blackboard eraser? |
|---|---|

## Pattern Practice

**7**

| It's | terribly<br>very<br>awfully | untidy<br>noisy | in here, isn't it? |
|---|---|---|---|

⬇

**8**

| It's much too | untidy for me to teach in.<br>noisy for you to hear me. |
|---|---|

⬇

**9**

| Please | tidy up,<br>settle down,<br>be quiet, | would you?<br>will you?<br>could you? |
|---|---|---|

**10**

<table>
<tr><td>Will you<br>Would you</td><td>all<br>both</td><td rowspan="2">straighten your desks,<br>tidy your desks,<br>put all your books/files/papers straight,<br>put that rubbish in the bin,<br>move your desk this way,<br>make a gangway through here,</td><td rowspan="2">please.(?)</td></tr>
<tr><td colspan="2">You need to</td></tr>
</table>

## Useful Expressions

| | |
|---|---|
| 좌석 정돈하기 | ■ We need to straighten up the room.<br>■ Let's line up our desks.<br>■ Move your desks forward(this way).<br>■ Would you make a bigger space here?<br>■ Would you please straighten the chairs?<br>■ Please arrange your chairs to make groups of 4.<br>■ Please move your desks this way. The aisle on your left side is narrow. Move them a little more. Now, it looks a lot better.<br>■ Move your desks forward(this way). Those sitting at the back, please move forward too. You look too far away. Can you hear me?<br>■ Please go ahead and arrange your chairs to make groups of 6. Please sit in a circle so that you can see each other. Move! Double quick!<br>■ Before we start the class, let's line up our desks. Third column from the window, would you move a little to the left, so I can walk between the aisles.<br>■ Why is it so noisy? Didn't you hear the bell? Hurry! Get back to your seats and get ready for class. If you behave like this again next class, you will be in a big trouble. I mean it. |
| 책상 위 정리하기 | ■ Would you mind cleaning up your desks?<br>■ Please put away things you don't need right now, so that they don't distract you. Let's do it now.<br>■ Put your things in your personal lockers, please.<br>■ Don't leave your personal belongings unattended.<br>■ And one more thing. Never ever put anything in the traffic area. Somebody will stumble or fall.<br>■ Please don't put breakable things such as cups or mirrors on your desks. While cleaning up the classroom or moving your desks, you could break them. You could also get a splinter. Please be careful. |
| 교실 청결 확인하기 | ■ The classroom is quite untidy.<br>■ Please, pick up all the things on the floor.<br>■ Please empty the wastebasket.<br>■ The curtains are so dirty. When were they washed last? |

| | |
|---|---|
| 교실 청결 확인하기 | ■ It's quite messy here. Look around and pick up the trash nearest you. You need to keep the classroom clean.<br>■ Who broke the window? If you break it, you pay for it. Who did this?<br>■ Why are the windows so dirty? Can't you see the fingerprints here? What about the dirty marks?<br>■ After this class, please make it crystal clear.<br>■ Jin-Young, would you pick up the garbage and put it in the trash can?<br>■ Everybody! Clean your work space.<br>■ There is dust all over the window ledge. You need to dust it. I will come back in an hour and check it. If it is still dusty, there will be trouble. |

## (2) 교실환경 확인하기 (Checking Physical Conditions in the Classroom)

교실의 공기가 답답하거나 이상한 냄새가 났을 때 환기를 시키고, 교실이 너무 덥거나 추울 때 실내 온도를 조절한다. 또한 조명이 너무 어두울 때 교실 조명을 조절함으로써 쾌적한 물리적 교실 환경을 조성한다.

### Dialogue Practice ①

T: What's that the smell in here? What did you eat?

Ss: Sorry, we had a hamburger during the break.

T: It smells horrible. Let's ventilate the classroom.
Will you open the windows?

Ss: It's too cold to open the windows.

T: OK. Let's open them for only 5 minutes. Guys by the windows, all stand up and open the windows, please.

Ss: All right.

## Dialogue Practice ②

T: Good evening, everyone. Don't you think it's cold in here? It's dark as well, isn't it?

S: It's always cold in here.

T: I'm afraid it is. Mee-Young, would you mind turning that heater up please? Yes, up! And, ...er Ji-Sun, will you check that heater next to you? Is it on? Myung-Su, turn those lights on, would you? Thank you... OK. That's better.

## Pattern Practice

**1**

| | | | | |
|---|---|---|---|---|
| It's | rather<br>a bit<br>too<br>very | hot<br>sunny<br>bright<br>stuffy<br>cold<br>dark<br>draughty | in this room,<br>in here, | isn't it? |

*Ans)* (Yes, it is.)
(No, it's OK.)
(No, it's alright.)

**2**

| | | |
|---|---|---|
| Isn't it rather<br>Don't you think it's too | sunny<br>hot<br>cold<br>dark | in here? |

*Ans)* (Yes, it is, rather.)
(I think it's alright.)
(It's alright for me.)

**3**

| | | |
|---|---|---|
| Isn't it too | hot?<br>cold?<br>dark? | Are you OK?<br>Can you work alright?<br>Can you see alright? |

**4**

<table>
<tr><td>Please</td><td>would<br>could<br>can<br>will</td><td>you<br>someone</td><td>turn<br>switch<br>put</td><td>the lights<br>the cooler<br>the air conditioner<br>the fan<br>the heater<br>the fire<br>the radiators</td><td>on?<br>off?</td></tr>
</table>

*Ans)* (I will.)
(I'll do it.)
(I can.)

**5**

<table>
<tr><td>We need<br>I think we need<br>I don't think we need<br>We don't need<br>Don't we need</td><td>the light<br>the lights<br>the cooler<br>the heater</td><td>on.</td></tr>
</table>

⬇

**6**

<table>
<tr><td>Will<br>Could<br>Can</td><td>you<br>someone</td><td colspan="2">turn<br>switch<br>put</td><td rowspan="2">it<br>them</td><td rowspan="2">on,<br>off,</td><td rowspan="2">please?</td></tr>
<tr><td>Would</td><td>you<br>somebody</td><td>mind</td><td>turning<br>switching<br>putting</td></tr>
</table>

*Ans)* (Alright.)
(I'll do it.)
(I will.)

⬇

**6**

<table>
<tr><td>Then<br>So</td><td>we can<br>we'll be able to<br>we can</td><td>see better.<br>keep warm.<br>cool.</td></tr>
</table>

**7**

<table>
<tr><td rowspan="2">Would<br>Could</td><td rowspan="2">you</td><td>open<br>close<br>shut</td><td>a window,<br>the window nearest you,<br>the door,<br>the shutters,</td><td rowspan="2">please?</td></tr>
<tr><td colspan="2">draw the curtains,<br>let the blinds down,</td></tr>
</table>

**8**

<table>
<tr><td rowspan="2">Would you mind if</td><td>we had<br>I switched</td><td colspan="2">the heat on?<br>the heater off?<br>the lights on?</td></tr>
<tr><td>we had</td><td>the door<br>the windows</td><td>open?</td></tr>
</table>

*Ans)* (No, that's a good idea.)
(No, that'd be fine.)

**9**

| Please, | could you<br>would you<br>will you | go and | ask<br>get | someone<br>somebody<br>Mr. Kim | to fix<br>to mend<br>to see to | the | light?<br>heater?<br>cooler? |
|---|---|---|---|---|---|---|---|

**10**

<table>
<tr><td rowspan="2">Oh!</td><td rowspan="2">Good.<br>That's nice.<br>Well done.</td><td colspan="2">You've remembered to</td><td>tidy up<br>open the windows</td><td rowspan="2">today!</td></tr>
<tr><td>What a nice and</td><td>warm<br>cool<br>tidy</td><td>classroom,</td></tr>
</table>

## Useful Expressions

<table>
<tr><td>교실 환기하기</td><td>■ It's stuffy here, would you open the windows?<br>■ One window is hard to open.<br>■ Could you open the windows to let the air in?<br>■ Will you open the windows? We need some fresh air.<br>■ Isn't it stuffy here? Please open the curtains and the windows to let some fresh air in.</td></tr>
<tr><td>교실 온도 확인하기</td><td>■ It's too warm/hot/cold in here.<br>■ How do you feel? Too warm? Too cold?<br>■ Isn't it too hot in here? Would you please open the windows?<br>■ Would you mind turning the heater on/off?<br>■ Can you turn the air conditioner on/off/up/down?</td></tr>
</table>

| | |
|---|---|
| 조명 조절하기 | ■ It's too dark/bright in here.<br>■ Will you turn the lights on/off?<br>■ Would you mind turning the lights on/off?<br>■ Can you close/draw the curtains/blinds?<br>■ The sun is too bright. Please draw the curtains.<br>■ The room is getting rather dark. Turn on the lights, please.<br>■ Please close the curtains. There is too much sun on the window side. I am showing a movie this class, so we need it a little dark. You can see it better.<br>■ It is rather dark today. Can the students over there read what I am writing on the board? Should I write in bigger?<br>■ It is cloudy today. I think you will have trouble seeing what I write. Should I write darker? |

## 4) 학습 전 활동 (Introduction of the Stages of the Lesson)

### (1) 복습하기 (Reviewing)

본 수업을 시작하기 전 지난 시간에 무엇을 배웠는지 묻고 대답하여 수업의 연계성을 갖는다.

#### Dialogue Practice ①

T: Let's go over what we did last class.
What did we talk about last time?

S: Passive and active sentences.

T: Right. Who can change this active sentence into passive one?
Can you do it, Na-Yeong?

S: Yes, it is "This book was written by Shakespeare".

T: Excellent! Let's begin today's lesson.

## Dialogue Practice ②

T: Before we start today's lesson, let's talk about what we learned last class. Chul-Min, can you tell me what we learned?

S: We studied nouns. There are countable and uncountable nouns.

T: Good job. Jin-Gyeong, what else did we learn?

S: We also studied how to say certain amount of water, coffee, paper, etc. For example, a glass of water, a cup of coffee and a piece of paper.

T: Excellent!

## Pattern Practice

**1**

| | | | |
|---|---|---|---|
| Where | did we | stop<br>finish<br>finish reading | last time?<br>last class? |
| | were we | | |

**2**

| | | | | |
|---|---|---|---|---|
| Who can<br>Can anyone | remember<br>tell me | what we | did<br>talked about<br>read about<br>wrote about<br>learned<br>used | last lesson?<br>last time? |

**3**

| | | |
|---|---|---|
| Do you remember | this?<br>these pictures?<br>this dialogue? | Listen. Who is speaking?<br>Look. |

**4**

| | | | |
|---|---|---|---|
| We | did this last lesson,<br>used these pictures,<br>practised a dialogue about ______, | didn't we? | Look! Listen!<br>Let's take a look again. |

**5**

| | | |
|---|---|---|
| Let's | go over it again,<br>revise it,<br>do it, | shall we? |

| 6 | | | |
|---|---|---|---|
| | How about<br>What about | doing it again quickly?<br>revising it?<br>going over it again? | OK?<br>Alright? |

### Useful Expressions

| | |
|---|---|
| 진도 확인하기 | ■ Where did we stop last time?<br>■ Where did we finish?<br>■ Where did we finish reading last time?<br>■ What were we?<br>■ What were we talking about last time?<br>■ Do you remember where we were? |
| 복습하기 | ■ Let's review the last lesson.<br>■ Let's go over our last lesson.<br>■ Last time we learned about relative clauses. |
| 배운 내용 물어보기 | ■ Do you remember this word?<br>■ Who can remember what we did?<br>■ Who remembers what we did last class?<br>■ Do you remember what we did last time?<br>■ Can anybody tell me what we did last time? |

## (2) 과제 점검하기 (Checking Homework)

지난 시간에 내준 숙제를 학생들이 했는지 확인하기 위해 교실을 돌아다니면서 검사하거나 과제를 수합한다.

### Dialogue Practice ①

T: Now, I'll check up your homework.
Everyone, please hand it in.
(Sudents pass their homework forward)
Did you all turn in your homework?

S: Miss Kim. I'm sorry. I forgot to bring it.

May I submit it next class?

T: Well, OK. But, I'll deduct one point.

## Dialogue Practice ②

T: I'm going to come around to look at your homework.

Everyone, please take out your notebook and open it.

S: Miss Kim. I'm sorry. I didn't know there was homework.

I was absent last class.

T: Well, OK. But, you should have asked your partner.

## Pattern Practice

**1**

| | | | |
|---|---|---|---|
| Everyone, | hand in<br>send up<br>submit | your homework. | Will you pass it up to the front? |

**2**

| | | | |
|---|---|---|---|
| I | am going to<br>want to<br>'d like to | check<br>collect | your homework.<br>your papers. |

## Useful Expressions

| | |
|---|---|
| 과제 확인하기 | ■ You had homework. What was it?<br>■ I told you to read Lesson 1. Did you do that?<br>■ The homework was to write the story in your book once in your note book. Remember? |
| 과제 수합하기 | ■ I want to collect the assignments.<br>■ Will the last person in each row collect the homework?<br>■ Have you all turned in your homework?<br>■ Hand in your homework.<br>■ Will you please send it up now?<br>■ Pass the sheets to the front.<br>■ Hand in your papers as you leave.<br>■ Make sure your names are on your work. |

## (3) 학습 목표 제시하기 (Presenting Aims)

학습 목표를 제시하여 학생들이 수업시간에 무엇을 배울지 알고 수업에 임하도록 한다. 공부할 내용과 학습 목표를 알려주고 따라 읽게 함으로써 학생들이 더욱 수업에 집중할 수 있도록 한다.

### Dialogue Practice ①

T: Today, we are going to learn some expressions that you can use to ask other's opinion. Look at the screen, and let's read today's learning aims.

Ss: (read the learning aims)

T: Good job. First, here are some expressions to ask others' opinion. After learning them, you will make a dialogue using those expressions. And then, I want you to role play with your own dialogue. When we've finished this, you will be able to easily ask others for their opinion. Let's start.

Ss: OK.

### Dialogue Practice ②

T: Who likes to go shopping?

Ss: Me!!

T: Obviously, everyone likes shopping. Personally I like it and so does my friend Su-Jin. Su-Jin is my best friend and she is studying in the U.S.A. When you go shopping in the US, there are some key expressions that you should know. Here's what we are going to study today. We're going to study those expressions and help my friend, Su-Jin, to buy a pair of sandals.

## Pattern Practice

**1**

| | | |
|---|---|---|
| By the end of this lesson you'll | be able to<br>have learnt<br>how to | say what you and your friends like doing.<br>talk about your likes and dislikes.<br>give descriptions of people.<br>use the present perfect.<br>give people advice.<br>warn people about dangerous things.<br>write a letter applying for a job.<br>discuss plans for a holiday. |

| | |
|---|---|
| Like<br>As in<br>For example<br>Such as<br>Look, like this | 'I love playing football but I don't like swimming much.'<br>'Well, he's very tall and slim, with fair hair.'<br>'If I were you, I'd buy the better quality one.'<br>'Have you finished that job yet?'<br>'Watch out! Mind that truck!' |

**2**

| | | |
|---|---|---|
| First<br>Then<br>Later (on)<br>In a few minutes<br>In half an hour<br>Half way through the lesson<br>Near the end of the lesson<br>At the end of the lesson<br>When we've finished this<br>Now,<br>Right now, | we're going to<br>I want you to<br>perhaps we'll<br>if there's time, we'll<br>if you've been good, we'll | practise this.<br>learn a dialogue about ___.<br>practise asking questions about ________.<br>learn something new.<br>make up a story.<br>listen to a lecture.<br>do some reading.<br>do some writing.<br>do some note taking.<br>have some conversation practice.<br>do some role play.<br>play a game.<br>sing a song. |

3

| | | | |
|---|---|---|---|
| Right.<br>Alright then.<br>Alright?<br>Ready? | Let's<br>We're going to<br>I want you to | | begin a new lesson.<br>listen to the dialogue.<br>read the text and find out the main idea.<br>do a drill. |
| | It's time | you | did something different/ new.<br>wrote a letter to your friend.<br>did a group project.<br>did some writing/reading/pair practice. |

### Useful Expressions

| | |
|---|---|
| 학습 목표 소개하기 | ▪ This is what we'll do today.<br>▪ Today's aims are that you will be able to apologize other people.<br>▪ By the end of this class, you will be able to say what you and your friends like doing.<br>▪ By the end of this class, you will have learnt how to write a letter applying for a job. |
| 배울 내용 설명하기 | ▪ Today we're going to do three main things.<br>▪ Now today we're going to revise the dialogue we learned last time.<br>▪ Today, I want you to learn some expressions about sports and hobbies.<br>▪ By the end of today's lesson, you will be able to apologize to other people.<br>▪ We're going to learn how to apologize to other people. |

## 5) 수업 전개를 위한 가교활동 (Bridge to the Lesson)

### (1) 동기 부여하기 (Motivating Students)

재미있는 게임이나 노래 부르기, 학습과 관련된 그림이나 사진 및 동영상 보여주기와 같은 다양한 활동을 함으로써 학생들에게 학습 동기를 부여하고 학습내용에 대한 흥미와 관심을 유발한다.

## Dialogue Practice ①

T: Now we are going to learn a new chant.
It's "How much is it?" Let's begin with a slow tempo.
And gradually we will increase the speed. First just listen.
One, two, one, two, one two three four, one two three four.

*How much is it? How much is it?*
*Please tell me. Please tell me.*
*How much is it? How much is it?*
*Please tell me. Please tell me.*

T: Let's chant line by line. Repeat after me.
Very good. Now, let's chant all together.

## Dialogue Practice ②

T: Now let's play a game.
This game is called Hangman.
Have you played this game before?

Ss: Yeah! We love that game.

T: Good to hear that. Then, let's start.
I'll make seven blanks, can you guess the letters?

S: T!

T: You got it. This word has a 't' in it.

S: O!

T: Sorry, there's no 'o'.

## A. 게임을 통한 동기부여 (Games & Activities)

### Pattern Practice

**1**

| | |
|---|---|
| Now, | we'll play a guessing game.<br>let me introduce a new game to you.<br>How about a game of "Simon Says'?<br>let's have a quiz.<br>let's play a spelling/miming/guessing/counting game. |
| Do you feel like a spelling/miming/guessing/counting game now? | |

**2**

| | |
|---|---|
| The idea of this game is | to score as many points as possible.<br>to get as many cards as possible. |
| Do you feel like a spelling/miming/guessing/counting game now? | |

### Useful Expressions

| | |
|---|---|
| 게임 소개하기 | ■ Let's play a game.<br>■ What about playing the "Hot Seat" game?<br>■ It's time to play an interesting game. |
| 게임 규칙 설명하기 | ■ Take turns.<br>■ Do as I say.<br>■ Let me demonstrate.<br>■ I shall be the referee.<br>■ Heads or tails?<br>■ Who wants to play first?<br>■ Whose turn is it?<br>■ Do what I'm doing.<br>■ Let's switch the teams around.<br>■ You have three chances.<br>■ First, I'll tell you how to play.<br>■ Clap your hands three times.<br>■ Watch me carefully and copy me.<br>■ The first one to answer gets a point. |

>>> 'Hot Seat' game은 일종의 스피드 단어게임으로 그룹으로 나누어 한 학생에게 칠판을 등지고 의자(Hot Seat)에 앉게 한 후, 같은 그룹의 다른 학생들이 칠판에 제시된 단어를 설명하여 맞추게 하는 게임이다.

| | |
|---|---|
| 게임 점수 확인하기 | ■ The first team to get ten points wins the game.<br>■ Try to do it exactly the same way as I'm doing it.<br>■ When I say "freeze," I want you to stop and listen to my command.<br>■ I'll write scores on the board.<br>■ Two points for this group.<br>■ You lose a point if you answer wrong.<br>■ If your team wins the game, I'll draw/put/attach a star on the board.<br>■ How many points have you gotten/did you get altogether?<br>■ What was your final score?<br>■ You're the winner.<br>■ It's a tie.<br>■ The winners say "hurray" and the losers give the winners a big hand. |

## B. 노래와 챈트를 통한 동기부여 (Songs and chants)

### Pattern Practice

3

| | | |
|---|---|---|
| Let's<br>It's time to<br>We're going to | sing<br>learn<br>listen to | a new song. |
| | chant.<br>clap by the rhythm. | |

4

| | | |
|---|---|---|
| Repeat | the words<br>line by line | after me. |

### Useful Expressions

| | |
|---|---|
| 배울 노래 소개하기 | ■ Let's sing a song.<br>■ It's time to sing a song.<br>■ Let's learn a new song today.<br>■ This song was sung by Britney Spears. |
| 노래 들려주기 | ■ Listen to the song carefully.<br>■ First listen carefully. |

| | |
|---|---|
| 노래 배우기 | ■ The song goes like this.<br>■ Listen and repeat.<br>■ Repeat after me.<br>■ Look at the third line.<br>■ Let's sing only the first verse.<br>■ Can you tell me what the word 'when' means? |
| 노래 부르기 | ■ Everyone sing all together.<br>■ Now you sing with me.<br>■ Sing along with me.<br>■ Who wants to sing with me? |
| 챈트하기 | ■ Now, let's chant.<br>■ Let's chant line by line.<br>■ Clap your hands with the rhythm.<br>■ Let's tap the rhythm together like this.<br>■ Let's chant in two teams.<br>■ Let's chant with motion. |

## C. 그림을 이용한 동기 부여 (Drawing and painting)

### Pattern Practice

5

| | |
|---|---|
| Can anyone guess<br>Can you tell me | what I'm drawing?<br>what this is?<br>what I'm holding?<br>what is on the screen?<br>what you are watching?<br>what you are listening to?<br>what the pictures on the book are about?<br>what the dialogue is about? |

6

| | | | | |
|---|---|---|---|---|
| Take<br>Have | a good look at the | poster.<br>picture.<br>screen.<br>projector. | What<br>Why<br>Where<br>How | do you think ___________? |

| 7 | | | | | |
|---|---|---|---|---|---|
| Look at<br>Tell me about | the | people<br>buildings<br>scenery<br>surroundings<br>section | on the left<br>on the right<br>in the middle<br>in the center<br>at the top<br>at the bottom | of the | poster.<br>picture.<br>diagram. |
| | | | in the top right-hand corner.<br>in the bottom left-hand corner. | | |

| 8 | |
|---|---|
| Now let's<br>I'm going to | take it down. |

⬇

| 9 | | |
|---|---|---|
| Can you remember | what | was happening?<br>happened?<br>had happened earlier?<br>was on the picture? |
| I want you to tell me | | |

## Useful Expressions

| | |
|---|---|
| 준비하기 | ■ Take out your crayons.<br>■ You will need some crayons.<br>■ I'm going to do an air drawing. |
| 그림그리기 | ■ Draw what I say.<br>■ Let's draw some pictures.<br>■ Listen and color the picture.<br>■ Everybody take one sheet of paper. |
| 색칠하기 | ■ Color the house red.<br>■ First, let's do some coloring.<br>■ Let's draw them on the book.<br>■ Color each balloon however you like. |
| 그림을 이용하여 학습하기 | ■ Guess what I'm drawing.<br>■ Follow my directions and draw what I say.<br>■ Draw a house inside the triangle.<br>* 삼각형: triangle * 정사각형: square * 타원: oval<br>* 직사각형: rectangle * 원: circle |

## (2) 페이지 찾기 (Finding the Page)

학생들에게 수업시간에 배울 교과서 페이지를 알려주고 주목할 필요가 있는 부분을 찾아 밑줄을 긋거나 표시하게 한다.

### Dialogue Practice ①

T: Now, open your books at(to) page 27. OK, last time we talked about the diagram on page 27. Do you remember what we discussed? Today we are going to start with the exercise on page 30. Now, I want you to turn to page 30, and have a look at exercise 1. It's on page 30. Are you with me, everybody?

Ss: Yes!

### Dialogue Practice ②

T: We've spent enough time on this.
Now, let's move on to the next page. It's page 167.

S: (students turn over the page.)

T: Here, we have some readings to do. The title of this article is...

### Pattern Practice

**1**

| Open | your books | to<br>at | page 56. |
|---|---|---|---|

**2**

| Turn to<br>Move on to | the next page. |
|---|---|

**3**

| Look at | the third line<br>the second column | from | the top.<br>the bottom.<br>the left.<br>the right. |
|---|---|---|---|

## Useful Expressions

| | |
|---|---|
| 페이지 찾기 | ■ Open your books, please.<br>■ Look at page 78.<br>■ Look at exercise 2A on page 62.<br>■ Use the index at the back of the book.<br>■ Have a look at the diagram on page 126.<br>■ You'll find the exercise on page 194.<br>■ Take out your books and open them to page 45/lesson3. |
| 페이지 넘기기 | ■ Turn over.<br>■ Turn to the next page.<br>■ Next page, please.<br>■ Let's move on to the next page.<br>■ I want you to turn to page 134.<br>■ Turn back to the previous page.<br>■ Now look back at the last chapter.<br>■ Keep one finger in the vocabulary list at the back.<br>■ You can refer to the map/list on page 216. |
| 학습할 요소 찾기 | ■ The line in the middle of the page.<br>■ It's somewhere near the top/bottom of the page.<br>■ It's towards the bottom/end.<br>■ It's about halfway down.<br>■ It's in the very middle of the page.<br>■ About three-quarters of the way down.<br>■ The top/bottom/middle line.<br>■ It's ten lines from the top/bottom.<br>■ Ten lines down/up.<br>■ The tenth line from the top/bottom.<br>■ The tenth line down/up from the bottom.<br>■ The third row down/up from the bottom.<br>■ It's on the right.<br>■ The left-hand side/the right-hand side.<br>■ It's in the top left-hand corner.<br>■ It's in the bottom right-hand corner.<br>■ It's in the left-hand margin.<br>■ Look at the right-hand column. |

| 학습할 요소 찾기 | ▪ The fourth word of the third line.<br>▪ The center/middle column.<br>▪ The shaded area on the right.<br>▪ The third paragraph, the second line/sentence.<br>▪ The last line of the first paragraph.<br>▪ The last line in the second paragraph.<br>▪ The third line, the fourth word along.<br>▪ Line five, the seventh word.<br>▪ About the middle of line 12. |
|---|---|

## 2. 수업 전개 (Development & Classroom Activities)

### 1) 모둠 만들기 (Dividing Up the Class)

#### (1) 짝과 모둠 만들기 (Pairs and Groups)

수업 활동을 위해 짝을 지어주거나 모둠으로 나누고 좌석을 배정한 후 책걸상을 이동하도록 시킨다.

**Dialogue Practice ①**

T: Now, I want you in groups. Groups of six.
So, look, you three turn around so you can talk to the three behind you.

S1: I don't understand what to do.

T: Look, turn around, so you can see Ji-Min, Sera and Ho-Sung.
Do you get it?

S1: Yes, I get it.

T: Good. All of you make groups like this one. You, six, you, six, you, six.

S2: Teacher, we're only four.

T: There are only four of you, I see. Well, four is fine. It doesn't matter.

## Dialogue Practice ②

T: In this class, we are playing a game. Listen carefully to what I say. I don't want to go over again.

Ss: Yes, sir. What kind of game are we playing?

T: I told you to listen. It is "Guess-the-Words" game.
First, please sit in groups of five. Move into groups.
Don't bang your chairs or desks. We don't want to disturb the class below.

Ss: Hey, let's hurry.

T: Now, you are sitting exactly as I told you. I have a lot of worksheets here. Each sheet has 20 words and you will explain them to your group in one minute.

Ss: That sounds quite challenging, ma'am.

## Pattern Practice

**1**

<table>
<tr><td>I want you in<br>We're going to work in<br>Can you get into</td><td>pairs.<br>groups.</td><td>In twos, with your neighbor.<br>In fours.<br>In groups of four.</td></tr>
</table>

**2**

<table>
<tr><td>Turn around<br>Move forward</td><td>and</td><td>face<br>look at</td><td colspan="2">your neighbor.<br>the person next to you.</td></tr>
<tr><td colspan="3">Can you face</td><td>the people</td><td>behind you?<br>in front of you?</td></tr>
</table>

**3**

<table>
<tr><td rowspan="2">You</td><td>are</td><td>by yourself,<br>on your own,<br>the odd one out,</td><td>aren't you?</td></tr>
<tr><td colspan="3">haven't anyone to work with, have you?</td></tr>
</table>

**4**

| | |
|---|---|
| Look, you<br>Why don't you | move up and make a three.(?)<br>turn round and join in with them.(?) |

**5**

| | |
|---|---|
| What about<br>How about<br>Would you mind | joining in with them?<br>going to sit there, next to him?<br>moving along a bit and working with them? |

**6**

| | | | |
|---|---|---|---|
| In your | pairs<br>groups | I'd like you to<br>you're going to | practise that dialogue.<br>try out some questions and answers about yourselves.<br>write a short paragraph about 'your family'. |

**7**

| | | | | | | | |
|---|---|---|---|---|---|---|---|
| All those<br>Those of you<br>Students | on the left,<br>on the right,<br>on this side, | you | are | Cathy.<br>Min-Su. | You<br>take | Cathy's<br>Min-Su's | part.<br>role. |
| | | | | group leaders.<br>You lead the discussion. | | | |
| | | | ask the questions.<br>give the answers. | | | | |

**8**

| | | | |
|---|---|---|---|
| When you've finished,<br>Then, | change<br>swap round<br>switch | so that you | take the other part.<br>each get a turn. |

**9**

| | | | | |
|---|---|---|---|---|
| OK.<br>Stop now! | That was good.<br>Not bad!<br>Well done! | Silence!<br>Quiet please!<br>That's enough! | Let's hear | what you've done.<br>this pair.<br>this group.<br>how you have been. |

**10**

| | | |
|---|---|---|
| Right. | Now A, you<br>B, you | ask the questions.<br>answer the questions. |

**11**

| | | | |
|---|---|---|---|
| We'll | keep score<br>write points | on the board and we'll see | who wins.<br>who gets the most. |

## Useful Expressions

| | |
|---|---|
| 짝 정하기 | ■ Get into pairs.<br>■ Work in pairs.<br>■ Get/Find a partner.<br>■ I want you to work in pairs.<br>■ Work together with a partner/friend.<br>■ Can you get into pairs?<br>■ You have no partner. I will be yours.<br>■ You are left alone. What about joining them ?<br>■ Turn around and look at your neighbor behind you.<br>■ Move around and face the person next to you.<br>■ I want you in pairs. In twos, with your neighbor.<br>■ You are by yourself, aren't you? Then I'll be your partner.<br>■ Work together with friends. |
| 짝 바꾸기 | ■ Please change partners.<br>■ Let's switch partners.<br>■ When you are finished, change over so that you take the other part. |
| 모둠나누기 | ■ In groups of four.<br>■ Let's make groups of four.<br>■ Let's sit in groups of four.<br>■ Let's make five groups.<br>■ Five groups of four, please.<br>■ Please get into groups of four.<br>■ Please get into five groups.<br>■ Each team should have four members/people.<br>■ I'll divide the class into five groups. |
| 자리 이동하기 | ■ Could you move your chairs/desks this way?<br>■ Move your desks back.<br>■ Move your desks over here.<br>■ Could you move back/forward a little?<br>■ This column move to the left. Those sitting in rows 1, 3, 5, please turn around. |

| | |
|---|---|
| 짝 활동하기 | ■ Try this in pairs. Don't copy down what your neighbor did.<br>■ Let's hear this pair. Would you say what you did again?<br>■ Watch me do it.<br>■ Don't disturb your neighbour.<br>■ Imagine yourself being the teacher. Ask your friend, "Who is your favorite actor?"<br>■ You are the teacher now. Ask the class, "What is this?" |
| 모둠 활동하기 | ■ In your groups, try some questions and answers about this dialogue. |

## (2) 전체와 팀 활동하기 (Choral, Individual and Teams)

반 전체가 한꺼번에 대답하도록 하거나 학생을 지명하여 개별적으로 응답하게 하여 학습 내용을 확인하거나 학급을 두 집단으로 나누어 활동을 할 때 쓸 수 있는 표현이다.

### Dialogue Practice ①

T: Right, I now want you to repeat parts of the dialogue. All together, (gesture), after me. Ready? Can I make an appointment for Monday?

Ss: (raggedly). 'Can I make an appointment with Dr. Lee for Monday'?

T: Oh, dear! That wasn't very good. Let's do it again. All of you, but keep together, and quietly! 'Can I make an appointment with Dr. Lee for Monday?' (gesture)

Ss: Can I make an appointment for Monday?

T: Better, good. Now, you, Kyong-Hee? Yes, by yourself.

S: er.. Can I make a appointment for Monday?

T: Fine, but an appointment and on Monday. Try it again.

S: Can I make an appointment with Dr. Lee for Monday?

T: Very good. Now in halves. (gesture) I'll divide you down the middle, here. Now, you (gesture) can ask and you, this side, can answer. So you ask 'Can I make an appointment with Dr. Lee for Monday?' and this side says, 'I'm sorry but she's all booked up on Monday. Could you come on Tuesday?' (gesture) etc.

Ss: Can I make an appointment with Dr. Lee for Monday?

Ss: I'm sorry but she's all booked up on Monday. Could you come on Tuesday?

## Dialogue Practice ②

T: Now, let's make sentences about the picture following the pattern: *'I saw ______ing.'* For example, we saw a girl watching the people outside.
(Showing a picture of two people playing tennis) Now, who can make a sentence?

Ss: Here. Teacher, here.

T: Don't shout out. Could you put your hands up before you answer, please?

S: Yes, teacher!

T: Ok, Su-Hyun.

S: We saw two men playing tennis at the court.

T: Great job. Let's give them a big hand!
So, who wants to do next? (Showing a different picture of a man swimming in the sea.) How about Sang-Hoon? Ready?

S: Yes.

T: Everyone, listen to Sang-Hoon.

## A. 전체응답 (Choral response)

### Pattern Practice

1

| | | | |
|---|---|---|---|
| I want<br>I'd like | all of you<br>you all<br>everybody<br>the whole class<br>this half<br>that half<br>one of you<br>just one person | to | answer the question.<br>repeat this sentence.<br>continue this sentence.<br>correct my statements.<br>read the next sentence. |

2

| | | | | | |
|---|---|---|---|---|---|
| No!<br>Oh dear! | That wasn't | very clear!<br>very good<br>all together!<br>loud enough! | Let's<br>Shall we | do it<br>try it | again. Ready? |

### Useful Expressions

| | |
|---|---|
| 전체 대답하기 | ■ Let's all say it together.<br>■ Like this, not like that.<br>■ All together now, please.<br>■ The whole class, please.<br>■ I want everybody(the whole class) to repeat this sentence.<br>■ Let's read the dialogue in chorus.<br>■ Now let's have someone else try it.<br>■ Everyone, listen and repeat what I say.<br>■ Don't answer the question until I ask you to. |

## B. 개별응답 (Individual response)

### Pattern Practice

**3**

| |
|---|
| Now one at a time. Not all together. Listen before you answer.<br>Don't shout out. Ready? Quiet. Listening.<br>You can take turns.<br>You can all have a go (a turn), but at a time.<br>One by one. Right? |
| Hands up before you answer!<br>Could you put your hands up before you answer, please? |

**4**

| |
|---|
| Now, this time, don't put your hands up. I'll point.<br>Everybody can try, but one at a time. I'll ask one of you. |
| Yes, a good answer. But a bit louder please. Again? |
| You can pick a girl for the next blank. |

### Useful Expressions

| 개별 응답하기 | ■ Try to work independently.<br>■ One after the other, please.<br>■ Say it with me.<br>■ Do what I'm doing.<br>■ Work by yourselves.<br>■ One at a time, please. |
|---|---|

## C. 순서 바꾸기 (Taking turns)

### Pattern Practice

5

| It's | his<br>her | turn | first,<br>second,<br>third, | then<br>now | it's your | turn. |
|---|---|---|---|---|---|---|

6

| Julie<br>you | first.<br>next. | Now | you.<br>Ben. | Quickly! |
|---|---|---|---|---|

7

| Whose | turn | was it?<br>is it? | Not yours.<br>It's hers/his. | Be quiet!<br>Come on! |
|---|---|---|---|---|

8

| Is it | Naeun | now?<br>next? |
|---|---|---|

| Come on!<br>Wake up! | wasn't<br>Isn't | it | his<br>your<br>her | turn? |
|---|---|---|---|---|

9

| Ok.<br>Alright. | Have you all<br>Who hasn't<br>Has anybody not | had a | turn | now?<br>yet? |
|---|---|---|---|---|

### Useful Expressions

| 순서 바꾸기 | ▪ Which team wants to do it first?<br>▪ The back row on its own.<br>▪ This row.<br>▪ Your turn, Bill.<br>▪ The next group.<br>▪ Just you, Alison.<br>▪ Take it in turns, starting here.<br>▪ Then you ask Min-Ji, and she asks Seon-Hee and so on around the class.<br>▪ Let's begin with the boys.<br>▪ Young-He. You go first. Next is you, Min-Ji.<br>▪ Isn't it your turn? Pay attention to what is going on. |
|---|---|

## D. 두 모둠으로 나누기 (Class in halves)

### Pattern Practice

**10**

| For this,<br>Now, | I'm going to<br>I'll | divide you down the middle.<br>divide you in half. |
|---|---|---|
| | this half of the class, you're A and, this half, you're B. | |

**11**

| Right. | Now, 'A', you<br>and you 'B', you | ask the questions, etc.<br>answer the questions, etc.<br>take the A/B part. | Then we'll<br>change over. |
|---|---|---|---|

**12**

| We'll | keep score<br>write points | on the board and we'll see | who wins.<br>who gets the most. |
|---|---|---|---|

### Useful Expressions

| 두 팀 활동하기 | ▪ Now I'm going to divide you in two halves.<br>▪ Let me divide the class into two. How can I divide it? Boys and girls? Odd numbers and even numbers?<br>▪ Girls only.<br>▪ These two rows. Please read A's part.<br>▪ I'd like this half to read the next sentence.<br>▪ I'd like this half to read the first sentence. And the right half to read the second sentence. And we keep the ball rolling this way until we are done the whole dialogue. |
|---|---|

## E. 팀 경쟁하기 (Team competing Activities)

### Pattern Practice

**13**

| OK. Now, | wait<br>listen | while I explain | how to play.<br>what we're going to do. |
|---|---|---|---|

| 14 | Which team can | answer<br>do what I say<br>do it | first?<br>best? |
|---|---|---|---|

| 15 | Remember your numbers. Well, | keep score.<br>see who gets the highest score.<br>see who gets the most points.<br>see which team wins. |
|---|---|---|

### Useful Expressions

| 팀 경쟁하기 | ■ Now we can have a competition, with teams.<br>■ For this, we're going to have teams, going from front to back.<br>■ 6 teams. Starting from here.<br>■ Each team! Please will you number off?<br>■ You're 1, you're 2 and so on. Number off, down the team.<br>■ Hands up, all number ones! Ready?<br>■ I'll call a number; only that number can do it.<br>■ We need you in pairs within your teams.<br>■ Each team, pair off.<br>■ In pairs, number off. |
|---|---|

## 2) 학습활동 (Learning Activities)

### (1) 듣기 (Listening)

학생들에게 듣기를 지도할 때 필요한 영어 표현이다. 듣기 활동을 안내하고 학생들이 쉽게 듣고 이해할 수 있도록 배경지식을 활성화하고 들을 내용을 미리 유추하고 질문을 던진다. 들으면서 그리기, 빈칸 채우기, 그림 맞추기와 같은 활동을 한 후 들은 내용의 요지나 줄거리 및 세부적인 질문에 답하도록 한다.

## Dialogue Practice ①

T: Before we listen to the dialogue, let's look at the picture on page 52. What can you see in the picture?

Ss: I can see a witch and Snow White.

T: Yes, there are two people. Where are they?

Ss: They are in Snow White's house.

T: What's happening? What are they doing?

Ss: The witch is selling a poisoned apple to Snow White.

T: Right. Now let's listen to what they are saying. Are you ready?

Ss: Yes.

## Dialogue Practice ②

T: Let me stop the CD for a minute. Did you hear any words you don't know?

S: What does 'watch out' mean?

T: It means 'be careful'.

S: Oh, I see. Thanks.

T: Now, I'm going to ask you some questions now.
Who can tell me the title of this story?

S: It's 'The country mouse and the city mouse'.

T: That's right. Which mouse said 'watch out?'

S: City mouse did.

T: Right. Who was coming to the room?

S: (no response)

T: OK, I'll play it again.
This time let's listen carefully to what the city mouse says.

## Pattern Practice

**1**

| | | | |
|---|---|---|---|
| We<br>You | will be listening to<br>are going to listen to | a section of<br>a part of | a story told by ____<br>a lecture given by ______<br>a conversation between ____<br>a news bulletin<br>a radio discussion<br>a phone call between ______ |

| | | |
|---|---|---|
| about ________, | and then | complete a worksheet.<br>discuss it.<br>answer some questions on it.<br>talk about it.<br>construct a flow chart from it.<br>write some notes on it. |

**2**

| | |
|---|---|
| This is to give you practice in listening for | the general idea.<br>the key points.<br>specific details.<br>relevant information.<br>the organization of the text.<br>the sequence of events. |

| | | | | | |
|---|---|---|---|---|---|
| And you | don't need to<br>probably won't<br>may not | understand<br>know | every | word.<br>phrase.<br>sentence. | It won't matter.<br>Don't worry. |

**3**

| | | |
|---|---|---|
| Who knows something<br>Who can tell us something<br>What do you know | about this topic? | What could the passage be about? |

**4**

<table>
<tr><td>Remember last</td><td>week<br>lesson<br>time</td><td rowspan="2">we learnt about</td><td colspan="2">different intonation patterns.<br>link words.<br>'marker' words like 'Well!'</td></tr>
<tr><td colspan="2">Don't forget what</td><td>words which introduce</td><td>an example.<br>stages.<br>a reason.<br>a list.<br>a change of subject.</td></tr>
</table>

**5**

| You're going<br>Are you ready | to listen and | answer these questions<br>fill in the flow chart | .(?) | I'll | start the tape.<br>begin reading.<br>begin talking. |
|---|---|---|---|---|---|

**6**

| Well. That's it. | We'll hear<br>I'll read | it again later, but | first check your answers. |
|---|---|---|---|

**7**

| Would | someone<br>one group | write their answers<br>put their solutions | on the board? |
|---|---|---|---|

**8**

| Do you | all agree?<br>think these are right? | Alright. Let's | go over that.<br>check your answers.<br>have your ideas. |
|---|---|---|---|

**9**

<table>
<tr><td rowspan="2">Now listen again and</td><td colspan="5">pick out the words which introduce ____.</td></tr>
<tr><td>notice how<br>tell me why</td><td>my voice</td><td>rises<br>changes<br>falls</td><td>when<br>after</td><td>I say.</td></tr>
</table>

**10**

<table>
<tr><td rowspan="2">Listen to this</td><td rowspan="2">sentence<br>short piece<br>extract</td><td rowspan="2">and pick out</td><td>a word<br>a phrase</td><td rowspan="2">which</td><td colspan="2">show(s) that ____.<br>mean(s) ______.</td></tr>
<tr><td>any words</td><td>denote(s)</td><td>color.<br>movement.<br>noise.<br>attitude.</td></tr>
</table>

**11**

| How else could | he have said<br>you say | that? | Could you | explain<br>say it | in your own words? |
|---|---|---|---|---|---|

**12**

| Could | anyone tell me<br>you in pairs tell each other | quickly<br>briefly | what | that was about?<br>might be said next? |
|---|---|---|---|---|

## Useful Expressions

| | |
|---|---|
| 듣기 안내하기 | ■ Listen carefully.<br>■ Let's listen to the dialogue first.<br>■ Let's listen again.<br>■ Can you hear me in the back?<br>■ You'll hear the following sentences. Listen carefully.<br>■ Before we study the reading part, I'll let you listen to the tape, first.<br>■ Listen to the tape looking at the pictures on page 20. |
| 듣기 전 질문하기 | ■ Before we listen to the CD, let's look at the picture on page 16.<br>■ What is this picture about?<br>■ What did you see in the picture?<br>■ What are they doing?<br>■ Where are they?<br>■ Where is the conversation talking place?<br>■ What is the relationship between the speakers?<br>■ What do you think they are talking about?<br>■ Why do you think so? |
| 듣기 중 활동하기 | ■ Fill in the blanks listening to the tape.<br>■ Please don't look at your book while listening.<br>■ You'll hear the following pairs of words.<br>Listen to the difference in sound.<br>■ Circle the right one among the given word after listening to the tape.<br>■ You will listen to a pair of words. Let me know if they are the same or different.<br>■ Listen and point the picture.<br>■ Listen and do what Minsu says.<br>■ Listen and draw what you hear.<br>■ Listen to Minsu and color your picture according to what he says.<br>■ Listen and put the pictures in order.<br>■ Listen and find the mistake.<br>■ Listen and put a check by the right picture. |

| | |
|---|---|
| 듣기 후 이해 확인하기 | ■ Let's see how much of the dialogue we understand.<br>■ What are Ji-Sun and Min-Su talking about?<br>■ What happened to Michael last night?<br>■ What is the problem?<br>■ Why can't Min-Su go hiking?<br>■ How does John help his father?<br>■ What do the speakers decide to do on Saturday?<br>■ Which team won the game?<br>■ Why is Tom happy?<br>■ What are they complaining about?<br>■ When is the train leaving?<br>■ What was the weather like on Monday? |

## (2) 읽기 (Reading)

학생들에게 읽기를 지도할 때 쓰는 표현으로 읽기 주제와 관련된 그림을 보여주거나 브레인스토밍, 마인드맵, 토의 등을 통해 주제에 친숙해지도록하고, 새로운 단어를 제시하여 본문을 이해를 돕는다. 본문을 소리 내어 읽거나 조용히 읽게 한 후 내용을 이해했는지 글의 요지나 세부사항을 질문한다.

### Dialogue Practice ①

T: Let's try something new before we read lesson 7. Let me write the title on the board.

(Teacher writes the title, *A New Friend,* on the board)

OK, everyone, Let's read the title together.

(Students read the title aloud with the teacher)

Good, What do you think this lesson might be about?

S1: How to make a friend.

T: OK, well, open your books to page 83. Let's look at the pictures and tell me what you see in the first picture. Min-Su?

M: A girl and a teacher are in front of the board.

T: Yes, They are speaking about something in front of the board.

Can you guess what they are doing, So-Ra?

S: I think the teacher is introducing the girl to her class.

T: Well, let's read the text and find out.

### Dialogue Practice ②

T: So you've all read it again, finished? Good. Now in pairs ask each other the questions under the text. Just questions 1-7. See if you can agree on the answers. One to seven. In pairs. In twos! Start now. I'll give you two minutes. (*Teacher wanders round.*)

Right, before we check your answers, I want you to answer my questions. Ready? Think, then put your hands up. In the first two lines, which words show you there is an example given?

S: Such as?

T: Do you agree? Is he right?

S: Yes.

T: Yes, good. Such as. So what is waste matter? Is it clean or dirty?

Ss: Dirty, old leaves, fish droppings.

T: Yes. Good. Right!

## A. 읽기 전 활동 (Pre-reading Activities)

### Pattern Practice

**1**

| | | | |
|---|---|---|---|
| I want you to read | the cards<br>these | out loud to me<br>silently to yourselves<br>to your neighbors<br>in your groups | and then... |

**2**

| | | | |
|---|---|---|---|
| Could you open your | reading books<br>textbooks<br>workbooks | and find | the story called '_____' in the index.<br>page 91.<br>the lesson we are on at the moment. |

**3**

<table>
<tr><td colspan="2">What does it say<br>Tell me what it says</td><td>at the</td><td>top<br>bottom</td><td colspan="2">of the page</td><td>.(?)</td></tr>
<tr><td rowspan="2">Look at the</td><td rowspan="2">exercise<br>writing</td><td colspan="5">in the middle.</td></tr>
<tr><td colspan="2">under<br>by</td><td>the</td><td>picture<br>photograph</td><td>on page 105.</td></tr>
</table>

**4**

| Can you read the instructions<br>What do you have to do | for this exercise? |
|---|---|

**5**

| You have to | match the questions to answers.<br>find the right word for each gap.<br>arrange the sentences into a good paragraph. |
|---|---|

**6**

<table>
<tr><td rowspan="2">Alright.</td><td>Do you all know</td><td>what to do?<br>how to read this?</td></tr>
<tr><td colspan="2">Does anyone have any questions?<br>Any questions?<br>Any problems?<br>Shall I go over it again?</td></tr>
</table>

**7**

| Right!<br>Ready? | What about<br>Look at | the | title<br>heading<br>picture<br>first sentence | .(?) | What | could it be about?<br>do you think it is about? |
|---|---|---|---|---|---|---|

**8**

| Have you ever | seen<br>heard of | this?<br>there? |
|---|---|---|

**9**

<table>
<tr><td rowspan="2">Before you begin reading,</td><td>you'll need to understand this word.<br>tell me what this word means.</td></tr>
<tr><td>look at this question.<br>make a note of these questions.</td></tr>
</table>

## Useful Expressions

| | |
|---|---|
| 표지, 삽화 등을 보고 주제 추측하기 | ■ Can you read the title together?<br>■ What do you see on the cover of the book?<br>■ What do you think this story is about?<br>■ What do you think will happen in this story? |
| 주제 관련하여 연상 질문하기 | ■ How many of you have been abroad?<br>■ Were there any difficulties in talking to people there?<br>■ How do you talk to people in other countries? |
| 지문에 쓰인 단어의 의미 확인하기 | ■ What does 'foreign' mean?<br>■ Are there any words you don't know?<br>■ Will you pronounce that word again, Insu?<br>■ There is an underlined word in the first sentence.<br>■ Check the new vocabulary from the list at the bottom.<br>■ I'd like to draw your attention to the word 'drag' in line 25.<br>■ It's worth noticing how the word 'sicken' is used in line 5.<br>■ I've just finished explaining some of the difficult words, phrases and sentences of this passage. Is there anything you don't understand? |

## B. 읽기 중 활동 (While-reading Activities)

### Pattern Practice

**10**

| | | | | |
|---|---|---|---|---|
| Read the | first paragraph<br>2nd section | silently | and | find the answer to this.<br>pick out the important points.<br>jot down the relevant information. |

**11**

| | | |
|---|---|---|
| Finished? | Then | discuss it/them with your neighbor.<br>write down a question to ask the class. |

**12**

| | | | | |
|---|---|---|---|---|
| Will you | think of<br>write down | some<br>2 | questions to ask | me?<br>your neighbor?<br>the other group? |

## Useful Expressions

| | |
|---|---|
| 읽기 시키기 | ■ Can you start reading for us, Bo-Ram?<br>■ Gun-Min, go on from where Bo-Ram left off.<br>■ Can anyone read this? Are there any volunteers?<br>■ Eun-Jin, you read the part of Mrs. Geller this time.<br>■ Now we'll read it again. Gun-Min, you can be Mr. Geller.<br>■ Let's try it again, but this time with Bo-Ram as Mrs. Geller.<br>■ Will you please read from the first line on page 80, Chul-Min? |
| 소리 내어 읽기 | ■ Read from line three to ten on page 70.<br>■ Read the lesson from the beginning to the end.<br>■ Read what it says at the top of the page first.<br>■ Let's read from the third line from the bottom on page seven.<br>■ If there is no volunteer, shall we select one or two speakers from our class? |
| 혼자 조용히 읽기 | ■ Read the chapter on your own.<br>■ You have five minutes. When the time is finished, you can use a dictionary to help you.<br>■ Read this passage as many times as you can in three minutes, then with your book closed, try to restate the ideas as clearly and completely as you can. |

## C. 읽기 후 활동 (Post-reading Activities)

## Pattern Practice

13

<table>
<tr><td rowspan="2">In line 4,<br>The 10th line from the top,<br>The 2nd line in paragraph 2,<br>Near the bottom,<br>The sentence beginning with "Today",</td><td>what</td><td>does the author mean by ____?<br>could he mean by ____?<br>do you think refers to?<br>does the word tell us?</td></tr>
<tr><td>Why does he</td><td>use the word 'moreover'?<br>repeat the words ____?</td></tr>
<tr><td colspan="3">Can you say/explain that in your own words?</td></tr>
</table>

<table>
<tr><td colspan="3">Let's recap quickly.</td></tr>
<tr><td rowspan="2">So what</td><td>do you think the author</td><td>wanted to tell his readers?<br>will say next?<br>will go on to say next?</td></tr>
<tr><td colspan="2">kind of people is the author writing for, do you think?</td></tr>
</table>

### Useful Expressions

| 지문의 이해 확인하기 | ■ What is the author's primary point about the topic?<br>■ Can any one of you tell us what the story is about?<br>■ Where is the thesis, in the beginning, in the middle, or in the end?<br>■ What's the main idea/theme of the story?<br>■ Who are the main characters?<br>■ What does Cinderella drop on the stairs?<br>■ Where does Tom go in the story?<br>■ Why is he angry?<br>■ How does she go home? |
|---|---|

## (3) 말하기 (Speaking)

수업시간에 배운 대화를 역할을 바꾸어가며 이야기 하고, 어떤 주제에 대해 토의할 때 쓰는 표현이다. 역할극의 역을 정해 연습한 후 다른 학생들 앞에서 시연하도록 한다. 토의 절차에 따라 주제를 알리고, 다음 단계로 진행하며, 토의가 끝나면 내용을 요약하고 마무리 한다. 자신의 의견을 분명히 표현하기 위해 이유나 근거를 제시하고 자신의 의견에 동의를 구한다. 의견이 다른 경우 상대방에게 정중하게 설명을 요구하고 피드백을 한다.

### Dialogue Practice ①

T: Settle down in your groups, now. Quiet, please! Look at this picture. What are these children doing?

S: Party.

T: Yes, they're having a party, aren't they? Well, today we're going to talk about parties. What are they eating and drinking? Can you see?

Ss: Coca Cola, Seven Up, sweets, cake, biscuits..

T: Yes, good. Why do you think they are having a party?

S: It's someone's birthday.

T: Great. How do you know that?

S: There is a big cake with many candles.

T: Excellent. Speaking of party, there will be a big birthday party for those who were born in July next class. How about planning for the party today?

Ss: Fantastic!

T: Ok. Then, let's think about the food first. I want you in your groups to decide which things you want for our party. You can discuss it, like this;

Let's have lemonade.

But I don't like lemonade. I like Coca Cola best.

Who else likes lemonade? No one?

Coca Cola then.

Shall we have some chocolates?

It's too hot. Chocolate might melt, and so on.

The group leader can make a shopping list, of four or five things, and we'll all look at them together. Off you go then. Group leaders, you start off: Ask your groups, 'What shall we have for the party?'

(Teacher walks round and listens, without correcting mistakes)

(Three minutes later)

Alright, everyone, let's compare lists, Jin-Joo, what's on your list?

S: Watermelons, cupcakes and gimbap.

T: Why do you want gimbap at the party?

S: All the members like it very much.

T: Oh, really? Then, can you tell me why you need cupcakes?

S: Because....

## Dialogue Practice ②

T: OK. Today we are going to discuss the differences between what is considered a First World country and a Third World country. Now I want you to consider the following statement: *First World countries have an obligation to help Third World countries with funds and assistance in cases of hunger and poverty.* Do you agree with this idea? Do you think rich countries have a responsibility for helping poor countries?

S1: Yes. This is true because of the First World's advantageous position attained by its exploiting the resources of the Third World in the past and present.

T: Do you agree? Any other ideas?

S2: You may be right, but not necessarily. The world economy is tough.

S3: Every nation suffers from economic recession and each country has its own business to mind. No matter how rich or poor, its responsibility is to feed and support its own people and develop its own economy.

T: OK, thank you for your opinions. Do you agree with S2 and S3? We have two opposite opinions. You are going to debate the correctness of First World countries' obligation to help Third World countries with funds and assistance in cases of hunger and poverty. Who supports extensive First World responsibility and who agrees with limited responsibility? Now, take a moment to think about your opinion and decide which idea you support.

Ss: Okay.

T: Alright, then. I want to divide you up into two groups based on what seems to be the opposite of what you really think. It is important to remember that you have been placed in your group opposite to your own idea. Do you understand? One group arguing for extensive First World responsibility, one group for limited responsibility.

## A. 역할놀이하기 (Role Play)

### Pattern Practice

1

| | | |
|---|---|---|
| We're going to do some role play now.<br>Listen while I tell you the situation.<br>Look at the picture while I explain. | Imagine<br>Suppose<br>Let's pretend | you are a president. |
| Now in groups of 4 think up what you can do. | | |

2

| | | | |
|---|---|---|---|
| I want you to | invent<br>think up<br>plan | a dialogue<br>a conversation | pretending you are these people. |

3

| | | | |
|---|---|---|---|
| What would you | need to ask<br>probably say | if you were | this man?<br>in this situation?<br>in the woman's shoes? |

4

| | | | |
|---|---|---|---|
| We're going to use | cue cards.<br>role play cards. | Each card tells you | who you are.<br>what kind of person you are.<br>which role to play. |
| | | On your card it says | what to do.<br>what you have to do. |

### Useful Expressions

| | |
|---|---|
| role-play<br>역할 정하기 | ■ Now let's act out this dialogue.<br>■ Now we shall act this conversation out.<br>■ Pretend that you're a pizza delivery man.<br>■ Imagine that you're phoning your brother.<br>■ Try and act like a bus-conductor.<br>■ Act as if you don't really care.<br>■ You are Mr. Smith, Min-Su and you are Mrs. Brown, Ji-Sun.<br>■ You can read the part of Mr. Smith.<br>■ You are the prompter.<br>■ You can be the reader, Ji-Sun. |

| | |
|---|---|
| role-play<br>연습시키기 | ■ Who would like to read the part of John?<br>■ Let's rehearse first.<br>■ Let's try it once with the book.<br>■ This will be our dress rehearsal.<br>■ You can use your book.<br>■ Try to manage without your book.<br>■ Take the parts indicated.<br>■ Each group represents one political opinion.<br>■ Take turns making offers and then refusing then.<br>■ Study your role and then work out a conversation.<br>■ Act as an interviewer and ask members of the class why they have applied for the job. |
| role-play<br>시키기 | ■ Who would like to act out the scene for us?<br>■ Who wants to be Alice?<br>■ Come out to the front and show everybody else.<br>■ Will the actors and actresses come to the front?<br>■ Let's watch Ji-Sun and Min-Su acting the conversation.<br>■ Let's see Ji-Sun and Min-Su's little play.<br>■ The rest of you are the audience. |
| 칭찬하기 | ■ I think we should clap.<br>■ Some applause for the actors and actresses.<br>■ Let's applaud the actors and actresses. |

## B. 토의하기 (Promoting Discussion)

### Pattern Practice

**5**

| | | |
|---|---|---|
| Why do you think | this man<br>the girl | looks happy?<br>is doing that? |

**6**

<table>
<tr><td rowspan="2">What</td><td rowspan="2">could<br>might</td><td colspan="2">have happened earlier?<br>have been happening?</td><td rowspan="2">Why do you think that?</td></tr>
<tr><td>happen</td><td>now?<br>in a few minutes?</td></tr>
</table>

7

| Now in | pairs,<br>twos,<br>groups, | prepare | a short story<br>to discuss what you think | about the picture. |
|---|---|---|---|---|

8

| Look at these pictures of | cars.<br>clothes.<br>furniture. | Which do you | like most?<br>prefer?<br>think are best?<br>like least? | Why? |
|---|---|---|---|---|

9

| Which<br>What kind of<br>Which of these | would you | buy for<br>give to | your parents?<br>your friend? |
|---|---|---|---|
| | | take with you | to school?<br>on holiday?<br>camping? |
| | | use at | home?<br>work?<br>school? |

Arrange them in order of preference.
Discuss your choice with your neighbor.
Persuade another that your choice is best.

10

| Now we've | read<br>thought<br>talked | about the problems of | pollution<br>traffic in town<br>choosing a career | together. |
|---|---|---|---|---|

| Can you discuss in | twos<br>pairs<br>groups | what you would do?<br>how these might affect you? | Write down | 5 things<br>6 ways |
|---|---|---|---|---|

| in order of importance. | And I'll come round and | see what you think.<br>help you. |
|---|---|---|

11

<table>
<tr><td rowspan="3">In pairs<br>In groups</td><td rowspan="3">I want you to<br>could you<br>can you work out how to</td><td>give someone else</td><td colspan="3">directions from school to.(?)<br>adescription of your school.(?)<br>instructions to use a copy machine.(?)</td></tr>
<tr><td rowspan="2">explain to someone</td><td>how</td><td colspan="2">rice is grown.(?)<br>Coca Cola is bottled.(?)<br>to operate a copier.(?)<br>to drive a car.(?)</td></tr>
<tr><td>what this</td><td>graph<br>map<br>diagram</td><td>shows.(?)</td></tr>
</table>

12

<table>
<tr><td rowspan="2">But first, let's</td><td colspan="3">do a practice round all together, so you know</td><td>what to do.<br>how to play.</td></tr>
<tr><td>go over some</td><td>words<br>phrases</td><td colspan="2">that might be useful.</td></tr>
</table>

13

<table>
<tr><td>We've got<br>There are</td><td>pairs of<br>sets of two</td><td rowspan="2">advertisements<br>maps<br>pictures<br>drawings<br>diagrams<br>house plans</td><td rowspan="2">which</td><td rowspan="2">are almost exactly the same.(?)<br>only have three things different.(?)</td></tr>
<tr><td colspan="2">Could you each draw two simple</td></tr>
</table>

14

<table>
<tr><td>You work in twos, with two similar pictures, but</td><td>don't let the other person see yours.<br>don't show yours to the other person.</td></tr>
<tr><td>Ask each other questions to</td><td>find out what is different.<br>discover what the differences are.</td></tr>
<tr><td>When you have found out,</td><td>write down the differences, and call me.<br>pass the two pictures on to another pair.</td></tr>
</table>

## Useful Expressions

| | |
|---|---|
| 토의 문제 알리기 | ■ Let's get started.<br>■ Let's start with the first question.<br>■ We need to discuss global warming.<br>■ First, we need to talk about our appearance-oriented society.<br>■ The first thing on the list is identity theft.<br>■ The first thing we need to discuss is bio-fuels.<br>■ The first item on the agenda is how to save energy. |
| 다음으로 진행하기 | ■ Let's move on to Item 2.<br>■ Let's move on to the next topic.<br>■ We need to move on.<br>■ The next item is the prohibition of cell-phones in school.<br>■ We need to go on to the next item. Shall/Should we move on?<br>■ Before we move on, I think we should think about First World obligations.<br>■ Wait a minute. We haven't discussed global warming.<br>■ Don't you think we need to help.<br>■ Not so fast. We haven't (yet) suggested any solutions. |
| 의견 제시하기 | ■ I think...<br>■ In my opinion...<br>■ I'd like to...<br>■ I'd rather...<br>■ I'd prefer...<br>■ The way I see it...<br>■ As far as I'm concerned...<br>■ If it were up to me...<br>■ I suppose...<br>■ I suspect that...<br>■ I'm pretty sure that...<br>■ It is fairly certain that...<br>■ I'm convinced that...<br>■ I honestly feel that ...<br>■ I strongly believe that...<br>■ Without a doubt,... |

| | |
|---|---|
| 설명 요구하기 | ■ What do you mean by First World Obligations?<br>■ I don't quite follow you.<br>■ I didn't get what you meant by cross-cultural understanding<br>■ Could you clarify that?<br>■ Could you elaborate on that? |
| 의견, 동의 구하기 | ■ What do you think, Ji-Hyun?<br>■ What's your opinion on that, Martha?<br>■ Any thoughts on that?<br>■ Any ideas?<br>■ Do we all agree (on that)?<br>■ Does everyone agree?<br>■ What should we do about it?<br>■ What needs to be done?<br>■ What do you think we should do?<br>■ What are we going to do about it?<br>■ Do you have any suggestions? |
| 제안하기 | ■ I recommend that ....<br>■ I would like to propose that ....<br>■ Why don't we ....<br>■ I think we should ....<br>■ Maybe we should ....<br>■ I suggest ....<br>■ Why don't we ....<br>■ How about ....<br>■ We could .... |
| 이유, 근거 제시하기 | ■ For this reason ....<br>■ That's the reason why ....<br>■ Many people think ....<br>■ Considering ....<br>■ Allowing for the fact that ....<br>■ When you consider that .... |
| 반대하기 | ■ Don't you think it would be better ....<br>■ I don't agree but I'd prefer ....<br>■ Shouldn't we consider ....<br>■ But what about .... |

| | |
|---|---|
| 반대하기 | ■ I'm afraid I don't agree....<br>■ Frankly, I doubt if....<br>■ Let's face it. The truth of the matter is....<br>■ The problem with your point of view is that.... |
| 피드백하기 | ■ (I think) that's a good idea.<br>■ You have a good point.<br>■ Good idea/point. I agree.<br>■ You can say that again.<br>■ That' a good point.<br>■ I agree with your idea.<br>■ I think you're right about that.<br>■ I disagree with your viewpoint.<br>■ You could be right, but I disagree.<br>■ Sorry. I don't agree with you.<br>■ You have a good point, but I disagree.<br>■ That's not such a good idea.<br>■ I don't think that's a good idea.<br>■ I'm afraid I can't agree with what you just said because…. |
| 요약 및 마무리하기 | ■ In summary,<br>■ The conclusion is ....<br>■ So, we've decided to ....<br>■ We're going to ... (then)....<br>■ I'll summarize by saying....<br>■ Are there any final questions? |

## (4) 쓰기 (Writing)

철자와 구두점에 맞게 단어 쓰기와 노트 정리, 문장 바꿔 쓰기 및 작문을 할 때 유용한 표현이다. 철자교정하기와 구두점에 맞게 단어 쓰기, 중요한 부분 노트정리하기, 문장 대체하기를 통해 다양한 형식으로 문장을 완성할 수 있도록 한다. 학문적인 글을 쓸 때 효과적으로 자신의 의견을 제시하고 다른 사람의 말을 인용하면서 반박하며, 인과관계를 설명하고, 결론을 내리고 자신의 주장을 요약하도록 한다.

## Dialogue Practice ①

T: What do you want to be in the future? I'm going to show you pictures of seven jobs. Let's write the correct job title for each picture. (After showing the pictures to the class) Did you all see them?

Ss: Yes.

T: Don't say the word. You're going to write it. Who wants to write on the board? We need three volunteers.

(Some students raise their hands.)

OK, Min-Hee, Sera, and Sun-Hee, come up here and write the job title. And the rest of you, write the job title in your notebooks.

(After the students are finished writing)

Let's see what you wrote.

Min-Hee, 'flight attendant', and Sera, 'flight attendant'. And Sun-Hee wrote 'flight attendant', too. OK, how many people had the same answer?

(Most of the students raise their hands) Right. 'Flight attendant' is correct. Let's go on to the next picture.

## Dialogue Practice ②

T: This is a sentence changing question. As you see in the example, you can change sentence patterns, by using "longer than" or "shorter than".

Ss: But longer is opposite to shorter.

T: Right. You should be careful with the subject. Read the sentences carefully.

Ss: "Your pen is longer than mine." and "My pen is shorter than yours."

T: Here is another thing to keep in mind. When you use these adjectives, please add "than" rather than 'to'. Also these adjectives don't need the comparative form, 'more'.

Ss: Yes, sir.

## A. 단어정의하기

### Pattern Practice

**1**

<table>
<tr><td rowspan="2">Before you</td><td rowspan="2">begin to write<br>do any writing<br>write anything</td><td rowspan="2">let's see if you can<br>I want you to</td><td>tell me<br>say</td><td>what you're going to write.</td></tr>
<tr><td colspan="2">do it orally first.<br>read this first.</td></tr>
</table>

**2**

<table>
<tr><td>Who can read this one?</td><td rowspan="2">Hands up<br>Put your hands up</td><td rowspan="2">if you</td><td rowspan="2">know.<br>can do it.</td></tr>
<tr><td>What does this say?</td></tr>
</table>

<table>
<tr><td>Can you</td><td>read<br>do</td><td>this one?</td><td>Everyone,<br>All of you,</td><td>put your hands up if</td><td>she<br>he</td><td>is right.</td></tr>
</table>

**3**

<table>
<tr><td rowspan="3">Careful!</td><td rowspan="3">This is<br>That's</td><td rowspan="3">a</td><td rowspan="2">new<br>hard</td><td rowspan="2">phrase.<br>word.<br>sentence.</td><td>Listen to how I</td><td>read<br>say</td><td rowspan="3">it.</td></tr>
<tr><td>Watch how I<br>This is how you</td><td>write<br>spell</td></tr>
<tr><td colspan="2">new exercise</td><td colspan="2">Watch how to do</td></tr>
</table>

**4**

<table>
<tr><td rowspan="2">You'll need<br>You need<br>Could you take</td><td rowspan="2">your</td><td rowspan="2">pens<br>pencils</td><td rowspan="2">out.</td><td rowspan="2">And<br>Also</td><td>your</td><td>note books,<br>exercise books,</td><td rowspan="2">please.</td></tr>
<tr><td colspan="2">some rough paper,</td></tr>
</table>

**5**

<table>
<tr><td rowspan="2">Match these<br>Make five good<br>Find ten true<br>Sort out these<br>Complete these</td><td rowspan="2">sentences, then</td><td rowspan="2">copy<br>write</td><td rowspan="2">them</td><td colspan="2">neatly.<br>carefully.</td></tr>
<tr><td>taking care with<br>and watch your</td><td>spelling.<br>punctuation.<br>capital letters.</td></tr>
</table>

6

| Check<br>It's | your | spelling of '______________'.<br>punctuation.<br>handwriting.<br>grammar.<br>capital letters. |
|---|---|---|

### Useful Expressions

| 단어 정의하기 | ■ Give the definition of each as shown.<br>■ Spell out the words that suit the given definitions.<br>■ Write the definitions of the words in English as shown in the example.<br>■ Spell out the word that suits the definition which follows. |
|---|---|

## B. 단어 철자 확인하기

### Pattern Practice

7

<table>
<tr><td rowspan="2">Make sure<br>See that</td><td rowspan="2">your</td><td>'g's, 'y's, and so on</td><td>sit on the line.<br>have tails which hang down.</td></tr>
<tr><td colspan="2">'k's, 'l's and so on go right up.<br>'u's are different from your 'v's.</td></tr>
<tr><td colspan="2">Don't forget to</td><td colspan="2">cross your 't's and dot your 'i's.<br>put capital letters where needed.<br>spell correctly.<br>write neatly.<br>lay it out neatly.</td></tr>
</table>

8

<table>
<tr><td rowspan="2">That's</td><td rowspan="2">quite good,<br>much better,<br>very neat,</td><td rowspan="2">but</td><td colspan="2">there's something missing<br>what's wrong</td><td>in this</td><td>line.<br>word.<br>phrase.<br>text.</td></tr>
<tr><td>you've</td><td colspan="2">forgotten something<br>left something out</td><td>here.</td></tr>
</table>

9

<table>
<tr><td>Is that a</td><td>true<br>good</td><td>sentence?</td><td rowspan="2">Can you read it to me?<br>Could you read what you have written, please?<br>Does it make sense, or is it silly?</td></tr>
<tr><td colspan="3">What do you all think?</td></tr>
</table>

10

<table>
<tr><td colspan="2">At home,<br>For homework,<br>Tonight,</td><td colspan="2">can you</td><td colspan="2">finish writing this?<br>write this out again neatly?<br>learn how to spell the new words?<br>practise writing ________?</td></tr>
<tr><td>and hand</td><td>your</td><td>books<br>papers</td><td colspan="2">in<br>to me</td><td>tomorrow morning by 8 o'clock.<br>next lesson, at ________.</td></tr>
</table>

11

<table>
<tr><td rowspan="3">Excuse me,<br>I'm sorry,<br>Teacher,</td><td rowspan="3">I didn't hear.<br>I don't understand</td><td rowspan="2">What</td><td colspan="3">are we doing<br>should we do<br>do we have to do</td><td rowspan="3">?</td></tr>
<tr><td>page</td><td>is it<br>are we</td><td>on</td></tr>
<tr><td colspan="4">How do we do it<br>Which books should we use</td></tr>
</table>

12

<table>
<tr><td rowspan="5">Excuse me,</td><td>Are these</td><td rowspan="2">alright<br>right<br>correct</td><td rowspan="4">?</td></tr>
<tr><td>Is this</td></tr>
<tr><td colspan="2">Have I done this alright</td></tr>
<tr><td>Is this</td><td>what you want<br>how you mean</td></tr>
<tr><td colspan="3">Why is this wrong?<br>I can't find any mistakes here!</td></tr>
</table>

## Useful Expressions

| | |
|---|---|
| 단어 수정하기 | ■ Correct the underlined part.<br>■ Give the correct form of the underlined part.<br>■ Point out the grammatical mistakes in the sentences below and correct them.<br>■ Give the proper form of the word in parenthesis.<br>■ Give(Write) the proper(correct) form of the given word (verb).<br>■ Change the verb in the parenthesis to its proper form for the sentence.<br>■ Complete the following with its proper verb form.<br>■ Cross out the word which is not suitable for the context.<br>■ Choose the suitable form of expression as you read the following passage.<br>■ Cross out the improper word for the context.<br>■ There are two words in the parenthesis. They are 'study' and 'to study'. Choose the right word to make the sentence grammatically correct. |

## C. 베껴 쓰기 (Copying)

## Pattern Practice

13

| | |
|---|---|
| When you've chosen<br>As well as choosing<br>After you choose | True, False or Not Stated,<br>the best order of the key points/sentences,<br>the best word for the gap, |

| | |
|---|---|
| I want you to write out | the true ones, and correct the false ones.<br>a complete paragraph.<br>a complete sentence filling the gaps. |

14

| | | | |
|---|---|---|---|
| So<br>First | let's practice orally<br>tell me exactly | what<br>the sentences | you're going to write. |

## Useful Expressions

| | |
|---|---|
| 베껴 쓰기 | ■ Copy this down in your notebooks.<br>■ You don't have to write this down.<br>■ Write it down at home.<br>■ Please summarize it in English.<br>■ Spell out the followings as you would read them. |

## D. 작문하기 (Writing)

## Pattern Practice

**15**

| | | | |
|---|---|---|---|
| Change<br>Put | the sentences<br>the verb | into | the passive.<br>direct speech.<br>the correct tense.<br>the singular/plural. |

**16**

| | | |
|---|---|---|
| Write<br>Change<br>Rewrite<br>Complete | the sentences,<br>the following sentences,<br>the passage, | using the passive.<br>leaving out the relative.<br>correctly punctuated.<br>using the words provided. |

**17**

| | | |
|---|---|---|
| Write<br>Summarize<br>Revise | an essay<br>the passage<br>the conversation<br>the lecture | of about 250 words.<br>in not more than 100 words.<br>in your own words. |

**18**

| | | |
|---|---|---|
| Kim (2000, p. 123)<br>In a study of …, Smith (2008, p. 333) | maintains<br>argues<br>asserts<br>claims<br>points out | that… |

## Useful Expressions

| | |
|---|---|
| 문장 고쳐 쓰기 | ■ Rewrite in the first person.<br>■ Change all nouns into pronouns.<br>■ Substitute 'too' and 'enough' for 'so' in these sentences.<br>■ Write the verbs in brackets in their correct form.<br>■ Change these sentences in the same way as the example.<br>■ Replace 'which' with 'that'.<br>■ Make these sentences passive.<br>■ Form adjectives from these nouns.<br>■ Complete the sentences with a suitable infinitive.<br>■ Complete the sentences by adding an article.<br>■ Complete the sentences, using the words provided.<br>■ Use one of the following words to complete the sentences.<br>■ Construct a suitable completion for the sentences.<br>■ Use appropriate forms of 'to be' to complete the sentences.<br>■ Insert the words given in brackets into the sentences.<br>■ Fill in the gaps/blanks, using the words given.<br>■ Put 'shall' or 'will' into the blank spaces.<br>■ Supply the correct form of the verb.<br>■ Supply the missing word.<br>■ Supply the missing articles.<br>■ Add the correct endings.<br>■ Fill in 'a' or 'the' where necessary.<br>■ Fill in the missing words in the following conversation.<br>■ Expand the notes below into complete sentences.<br>■ Combine each pair of sentences, using 'although'. |
| 문장 바꿔 쓰기 | ■ Rewrite in the first person.<br>■ Change all nouns into pronouns.<br>■ Substitute 'too' and 'enough' for 'so' in these sentences.<br>■ Write the verbs in brackets in their correct form.<br>■ Change these sentences in the same way as the example.<br>■ Replace 'which' with 'that'.<br>■ Make these sentences passive.<br>■ Form adjectives from these nouns.<br>■ Complete the sentences with a suitable infinitive.<br>■ Complete the sentences by adding an article. |

| | |
|---|---|
| 문장 바꿔 쓰기 | ■ Complete the sentences, using the words provided.<br>■ Use one of the following words to complete the sentences.<br>■ Construct a suitable completion for the sentences.<br>■ Use appropriate forms of 'to be' to complete the sentences.<br>■ Insert the word given in brackets into the sentences.<br>■ Fill in the gaps/blanks, using the words given.<br>■ Put 'shall' or 'will' into the blank spaces.<br>■ Supply the correct form of the verb.<br>■ Supply the missing word.<br>■ Supply the missing articles.<br>■ Add the correct endings.<br>■ Fill in 'a' or 'the' where necessary.<br>■ Fill in the missing speeches in the following conversation.<br>■ Expand the notes below into complete sentences.<br>■ Combine each pair of sentences, using 'although'.<br>■ Punctuate the following passage. |
| 작문하기 | ■ Write an essay of about 250 words on one of the following subjects.<br>■ Write an answer to Bill's letter. Begin: 'Thanks for....'<br>■ Summarize the passage in not more than 100 words.<br>■ Read the following passage and then answer the questions on it.<br>■ State Bill's reasons for leaving in your own words.<br>■ Now write an essay describing what you enjoy doing using the ideas below.<br>■ Now give opinions on the following topics and use specific reasons and examples to support your answer.<br>■ Write a letter which offers these people some advice.<br>■ Summarize the points made in the lecture, explaining how they cast doubt on the points made in the reading. |
| 주제 쓰기 | ■ The aim of this paper is to ....<br>■ The point of this essay is to ....<br>■ It shall be argued in this essay is that ....<br>■ The view presented in this review is that .... |
| 의견 제시하기 | ■ There are many reasons why ....<br>■ It is important/ necessary to point out that....<br>■ The first thing to be considered is ....<br>■ It is a fact that ....<br>■ There is some doubt that .... |

| | |
|---|---|
| 인용하기 | ■ The opinion of Smith (1999, p. 333) is that ...<br>■ Smith (1992, p. 123) has suggested that ....<br>■ According to Smith (1992, p. 123)....<br>■ It is thought by some theorists, for example, Jones (2004, p. 2) and Smith (2002, p. 1) that ....<br>■ Smith (2002, p.123) is certainly/may be correct/accurate in saying that ... because ....<br>■ As Smith (2002, p.123) says/states ....<br>■ Like Smith (2002, p.123), it can be agreed that .... because ....<br>■ Based on these authors, a connection can be made between....<br>■ It can be concluded from what Kim (2004, p. 2) and Smith (2002, p. 1) have stated that... is....<br>■ When Kim' s (2007, p.123) work/paper is looked at closely, it is seen that....<br>■ One outcome of Smith' s (2001, p.52) work/paper/research is .... |
| 다른 사람 의견에 반대하기 | ■ Kim (2008, p.123) fails to address the issue when he says '...' because ....<br>■ When Kim (2008, p.123) argues that.... His reasoning is questionable because ....<br>■ One of the main arguments against Kim (2008, p.123) is that ....<br>■ Kim's (2008) approach/ position is somewhat inadequate (in-accurate) because ....<br>■ Kim's (2008) methods are somewhat insufficient because ....<br>■ Although the research has tended to focus on ... rather less attention has been paid to....<br>■ Although most studies, such as Kim (2004, p. 2) and Lee (2002, p. 1), have emphasized/concentrated on/focussed on ... inadequate /insufficient .... |
| 부연, 첨가하기 | ■ The first/second reason why ... is ....<br>■ Firstly/ Secondly ....<br>■ The most important ... is ....<br>■ In addition, ....<br>■ What is more, ....<br>■ Another reason is ....<br>■ A further point is .... |

| | |
|---|---|
| 결론 내리기 | ■ It follows that ....<br>■ After quoting evidence you reach a conclusion that ....<br>■ The evidence seems to indicate that ....<br>■ It must therefore be recognised that ....<br>■ The indications are therefore that ....<br>■ It is clear therefore that ....<br>■ Thus it could be concluded that ....<br>■ The evidence seems to be strong that ....<br>■ On this basis it may be inferred that ....<br>■ Given this evidence, it can be seen that .... |
| 요약하기 | ■ In short, ....<br>■ All in all ....<br>■ I'd like to finish by saying ....<br>■ In brief, ....<br>■ In short, ....<br>■ On the whole, ....<br>■ To conclude ....<br>■ In conclusion, ....<br>■ As I have shown, ....<br>■ As I have said, .... |

## (5) 어휘 (Vocabulary)

새로운 어휘를 제시하고 단어의 뜻을 묻거나 문맥을 통해 의미를 추론한다. 단어의 뜻을 자신의 말로 설명하게 하고 어휘의 품사, 반의어, 동의어 학습을 통해 어휘지식을 확장하도록 한다. 문법적 기능을 지닌 어휘와 상황에 적절한 어휘 표현을 습득하도록 한다.

### Dialogue Practice ①

T: When you come up with unknown words while you are reading, what do you do?

Ss: Look up the word in a dictionary.

Ignore it and keep reading.

Guess the meaning in the context.

T: All right. When you want to understand a new word, use the context. It can tell you a lot about a new word. It can tell you what kind of word it is-noun, verb, adjective, adverb, etc. It can also give you some idea of the meaning of the word.

Now, everyone. Read the following sentence and guess the meaning of "taboo," and write the meaning in English. It doesn't have to be exact.

What is taboo?

Ss: Something that we are not likely to do.

Something we cannot do.

T: Very good. 'taboo' is something we must avoid because others do not like it. Then what helped you guess the meaning of taboo?

Ss: I read a news article and that said talking about one's income is a taboo because it can make others embarrassed.

T: Excellent. Likewise, you can guess the meaning of a word in a context. Now, I want you to think of what kind of word 'taboo' is. Is it a noun, verb, adjective or adverb?

Ss: It is a noun.

T: How did you find that?

Ss: There is "a" in front of taboo. It replaces with "it".

T: Perfect. Now, I want you to read the rest of the sentences. There is a word you probably do not know. Use the context to guess the general meaning of the word. Write the general meaning in English. For each item, you also write what kind of the word it is.

## Dialogue Practice ②

T: We're going to have a discussion today but first I want you to read a short passage about a businesswoman. She wants to keep fit. Who knows what "keep fit" means?

S: Sport? Something to do with sports?

T: Possibly, yes. Some people do exercises every morning to keep fit, to keep healthy, to keep their muscles in honed. If you are fit, you can run a long way. OK?

S: Yes.

T: Do you exercise sometimes?

S: Yes, I do.

T: Why? to ....?

S: To keep fit.

T: Good. She wants to keep fit. Now. Some people in Korea go to a fitness center and do some running and weight training every day. Weight training; Who knows what weight training means?

S: Maybe... Work out to lose weight?

T: Possibly. You work out with some equipment. And you lift weights and pull weights to strengthen your muscles. Weight training is a muscle-strengthening exercise performed with the aid of adjustable weights and pulleys. Who can spell it for me?

S: w-e-i-g-h-t t-r-a-i-n-i-n-g.

T: Good. Now I'll hand out the passage.

## Pattern Practice

### A. 새로운 어휘 소개 (Introducing the new words)

1

| | | |
|---|---|---|
| Here are | new words<br>new vocabulary | we don't know.<br>we haven't learned.<br>we haven't seen before. |
| Let's | take a look at<br>look at<br>check out<br>read through | the new words.<br>the vocabulary first. |

2

| | | | | |
|---|---|---|---|---|
| First,<br>Before we begin, | I want to<br>I'd like to | check that<br>make sure | you know | the meaning of a few words.<br>what one or two words mean. |

| 3 | | | | |
|---|---|---|---|---|
| I want<br>I'm going | to teach you<br>to explain | a few new<br>some useful | words that we shall need<br>expressions that we will use | later on today.<br>for a dialogue.<br>for a role play.<br>for reading. |

| 4 | | |
|---|---|---|
| Before you begin | reading<br>listening | you'll need to understand '____________'.<br>tell me what '____________' means.<br>could someone explain '____________'. |

## Useful Expressions

| 새로운 어휘 제시하기 | |
|---|---|
| | ■ Let's have a look at the new words.<br>■ I don't think you've had(met) this word before.<br>■ Let's try something new words before we read.<br>■ We're going to do the vocabulary before we read the text.<br>■ Here's a word we don't know.<br>■ Here's a word we haven't learned.<br>■ Here's a word we haven't seen before.<br>■ Discuss any words or phrases you don't know. |

## B. 의미 추론하기 (Making students guess the meaning)

| 5 | |
|---|---|
| Who knows<br>Does anyone know<br>Can anyone tell me | what this word means: '__________'?<br>when you would use the word, '__________'?<br>where you would see/hear the word, '__________'? |

| 6 | | | |
|---|---|---|---|
| I'll give you | a clue.<br>some help. | It's something to do with ____________.<br>You might hear a ________ saying it. | |
| Let's see if you can guess. | | I'll give you | the context: __________.<br>an example: __________. |

7

| Not really.<br>Nearly right!<br>Not quite!<br>Wait! | Listen to me and I'll<br>Watch me and I'll | explain.<br>give you another example.<br>show you.<br>draw one.<br>act it out. |
|---|---|---|

8

| Now look at the | picture opposite. | | What | does it tell you?<br>does the word 'snob' mean?<br>is the author talking about? |
|---|---|---|---|---|
| | sentence | before.<br>carefully.<br>after.<br>beginning with '______'. | | |
| So what could this word | | be about?<br>refer to?<br>mean? | | |

9

| Look!<br>Listen!<br>Watch! | Who knows<br>Does anyone know | what | this is<br>we call this<br>this person is doing<br>we say when ________<br>this does<br>this shows | in English? |
|---|---|---|---|---|

10

| If<br>Supposing<br>Pretend | I<br>you | had ________,<br>were ________,<br>lived in ________,<br>felt ________, | I'd<br>you'd | have to ________.<br>be ________.<br>need ________. | What? |
|---|---|---|---|---|---|

11

| Look at | the | title.<br>heading.<br>picture.<br>first sentence. | What could this word mean?<br>When do you think you would use this word? |
|---|---|---|---|

12

| Can you<br>Would you | say that<br>explain that<br>paraphrase that | in your own words?<br>in other words?<br>differently? |
|---|---|---|

## Useful Expressions

| | |
|---|---|
| 어휘 뜻 묻기 | ■ What does 'blue' mean here?<br>■ What does 'sang' refer to in this sentence?<br>■ What do the words in brackets/ italics mean here?<br>■ What does 'sang' refer to in this sentence? |
| 어휘 추론하기 | ■ In what sense is the word 'cry' used here?<br>■ Find another phrase/ expression that means the same thing.<br>■ Can you give me one word that means 'to come back'?<br>■ How else can you say the same thing?<br>■ What's one word that means/ for 'out of work'?<br>■ What's a shorter way of saying 'he went by plane'<br>■ What's a man who carries bags called?<br>■ What do you call a person who moves to another country?<br>■ What's the difference between 'stick' and 'racket'?<br>■ Give me a phrase that means approximately the same thing.<br>■ Give me a phrase that means more or less the same thing. |
| 다른 말로 바꿔 쓰기 | ■ Where can you see this phrase?<br>■ Write sentences to explain the following words.<br>■ Make sentences to show you understand the meaning of the following words.<br>■ Use your own words to describe what happened.<br>■ Use your own words to tell me about Susan.<br>■ Explain the meaning of this sentence, using your own words.<br>■ Tell me in your own words what happened.<br>■ Can you paraphrase this sentence?<br>■ Can you summarize the last paragraph?<br>■ Is there another way to saying the same thing?<br>■ Any alternatives for this word?<br>■ Could you phrase it slightly differently?<br>■ What other word could you use here?<br>■ Try to put it in other words.<br>■ Tell me when you use this word. |

## C. 어휘 확장하기 (Expanding a known word)

**13**

<table>
<tr><td rowspan="2">You all<br>know the</td><td rowspan="2">word ________.<br>phrase ________.<br>idea of ________.</td><td rowspan="2">OK. Well, what's</td><td colspan="3">the opposite of it?<br>another word for it?<br>the general form of it?</td></tr>
<tr><td>the</td><td>verb<br>noun</td><td>from it?</td></tr>
</table>

**14**

<table>
<tr><td>In this</td><td>context<br>sentence</td><td>for example, ________.</td><td>It begins with</td><td>A.<br>B.<br>C.</td></tr>
<tr><td>It is</td><td colspan="2">similar to ________.<br>something to do with ________.</td><td colspan="2">Take a guess!<br>What could it be?</td></tr>
</table>

**15**

<table>
<tr><td rowspan="2">What's the</td><td>noun<br>adjective</td><td>that is derived from<br>that corresponds to<br>that is based on</td><td rowspan="2">'prevent'?</td></tr>
<tr><td>word</td><td>opposite of<br>similar to<br>equivalent to</td></tr>
</table>

## Useful Expressions

<table>
<tr><td>단어 품사나<br>파생어 묻기</td><td>■ What is the noun derived from 'electric'?<br>■ What's the verb that corresponds to this noun?<br>■ What's the adjective that comes from 'nation'?<br>■ What's the noun of 'generous'?<br>■ Can anyone tell me the corresponding verb?<br>■ What's the prefix that means 'against'?</td></tr>
<tr><td>반의어나 동의어<br>묻기</td><td>■ Give a synonym for 'rushed'.<br>■ What are the words that are similar to 'preserve'?<br>■ What is the word that is opposite of 'save'?<br>■ What is a synonym of 'tightly'?<br>■ What is an antonym of 'big'?<br>■ What's another way of saying 'he shuttered'?</td></tr>
</table>

<table>
<tr><td>반의어나 동의어 묻기</td><td>■ What's another word that means the opposite as 'huge'?<br>■ What are two words that mean the same as 'tripped'?<br>■ What's the word that rhymes with 'blue' meaning 'a hint' or 'tip'?<br>■ It's a synonym of/for 'jealous'.</td></tr>
</table>

## D. 연결어와 문법적 기능을 가진 어휘 지도하기 (Teaching 'link' words and words with a grammatical function)

16

<table>
<tr><td rowspan="2">In line 5, what does this word</td><td>'however'<br>'although'<br>'alternatively'</td><td>tell you about what follows?</td></tr>
<tr><td>'them'<br>'which'<br>'this'</td><td>refer to?</td></tr>
</table>

17

<table>
<tr><td rowspan="2">In line 2,<br>The 8th line from the top,<br>The 1st line paragraph 2,<br>Near the bottom,<br>In the sentence beginning with 'Compared',</td><td>what</td><td>does the author mean by 'in a nutshell'?<br>could he mean by 'otherwise'?<br>do you think 'which' refers to?<br>does the word 'however' tell us?</td></tr>
<tr><td>why does he</td><td>use the word 'moreover'?<br>repeat the words 'besides'?</td></tr>
</table>

18

<table>
<tr><td rowspan="2">Look. The word</td><td>ends in</td><td>'tion'<br>'ness'</td><td>so it must be a noun.</td></tr>
<tr><td colspan="3">begins with 'un' so it means 'not' something.</td></tr>
</table>

19

<table>
<tr><td>It's</td><td>big and<br>made of ______</td><td rowspan="2">It's used for ______ing things, when they ______.<br>People use it to ____________.<br>You can ____________ it.</td></tr>
<tr><td colspan="2">You see it in _____s</td></tr>
</table>

## Useful Expressions

| | |
|---|---|
| 연결 단어나 문법적 기능을 지닌 어휘 묻기 | ■ Can we leave this conjunction out?<br>■ Combine each pair of sentences, using 'although.'<br>■ What does the relative pronoun refer to?<br>■ Do we need the relative here?<br>■ Which preposition comes after 'to concentrate'?<br>■ Which tense do we use after 'if'?<br>■ What's the rule about 'some' and 'any'?<br>■ Does anybody recall what we said about the verb 'to dare'?<br>■ What's the past tense of 'to go'?<br>■ What part of speech is 'to sing'?<br>■ What are the frequency adverbs?<br>■ What kinds of adjective words do you use when you describe someone's appearance?<br>■ What adverbs are used when you describe motion?<br>■ Where do we usually put adverbs of frequency?<br>■ Where do you put conjunction in this sentence?<br>■ Where does the word 'yet' usually come? |
| 단어를 이용하여 문장 완성시키기 | ■ Choose the verb that best fits each sentence.<br>■ Put a circle around the best alternative.<br>■ Choose the correct completion for each sentence.<br>■ You have to include the preposition.<br>■ The preposition has to be kept in.<br>■ They're spelt the same, but pronounced differently.<br>■ Supply the correct form of the verb.<br>■ Complete the sentences by adding an article or making a noun plural.<br>■ Insert the words given in brackets into the sentences.<br>■ Add correct endings.<br>■ Choose the verb that best fits each sentence. |

## E. 적절한 어휘사용 지도하기 (Teaching appropriate vocabulary use)

**20**

| | | | |
|---|---|---|---|
| '_____' | is<br>sounds | a bit too<br>rather<br>very | formal.<br>informal.<br>colloquial.<br>old fashioned. |

| | | | | | |
|---|---|---|---|---|---|
| You | only<br>should | use<br>say | '_________' | if you're talking to friends.<br>talking to your boss.<br>writing a formal letter.<br>writing to friends. | |
| | | | | with people you | don't know.<br>know very well. |

### Useful Expressions

| | |
|---|---|
| 상황에 적절한 어휘 표현하기 | ■ It sounds better to say 'I apologize.'<br>■ Can we say it in another way? It sounds too formal.<br>■ That is all right, but is there another way to say it more politely?<br>■ What you said isn't wrong, but 'To Whom It May Concern' sounds more formal.<br>■ It might be better to say 'How are you, sir? in this context.<br>■ I think 'then he left' sounds better in this sentence.<br>■ An Englishman would probably say 'Oh, my goodness' instead of 'Oh, my God'. |

## F. 이해 확인하기 (Checking students' understanding)

**21**

| | |
|---|---|
| Spell it<br>It's spelt<br>Write it | with an 'i' and then and 'e'.<br>with two 's's, not one.<br>with a capital letter.<br>with small letters. |

**22**

| | |
|---|---|
| I'm afraid,<br>I'm sorry, | this is spelt wrong.<br>you've made a spelling mistake.<br>there are two words you've spelt wrong.<br>you've slipped up over/on two words. |

## Useful Expressions

| | |
|---|---|
| 철자 교정하기 | ■ What letter is missing?<br>■ Is this letter right/correct?<br>■ Spell it with an 'i' and then and 'e'.<br>■ There's a 'k' missing.<br>■ A 'k' is missing.<br>■ 'K' is missing.<br>■ There's one letter two many/few.<br>■ You've got one 'l' too many/few.<br>■ It's spelt with two 'p's, not one.<br>■ Double 's's.<br>■ You need an extra letter here.<br>■ There should be an 'o' instead of a 'u'.<br>■ Write it with a capital 'J'.<br>■ Spell it with small letters.<br>■ The word ends/begins with the letter 'p'.<br>■ It begins with a 'j'.<br>■ Write it as one word/two words.<br>■ Write them separately/ together.<br>■ These two letters are the wrong way round.<br>■ The word is spelt 'c-o-n-s-c-i-o-u-s'. |
| 철자 확인하기 | ■ Have you spelt it right?<br>■ Let's see if you've spelt it right/correctly.<br>■ Is there anything wrong with the spelling?<br>■ Can anybody correct Ji-sun's spelling?<br>■ I'm afraid this is spelt wrong.<br>■ I'm sorry, you've made a spelling mistake.<br>■ There are two words you've spelt wrong.<br>■ You've slipped up over/on two words. |
| 이해 확인하기 | ■ Find English words that mean the same as ________.<br>■ Explain the meaning of the following words, as used in the passage.<br>■ Explain the meaning in English of the following words.<br>■ Supply the missing word.<br>■ Match the word with the picture.<br>■ Match the word with the definition.<br>■ Make a sentence with the following words.<br>■ Solve the crossword puzzle.<br>■ Fill in the gaps/ blanks, using the words given.<br>■ Expand the notes below into complete sentences. |

## 3) 학습지와 기자재 사용 (Handouts & Multimedia Equipment)

### (1) 학습지 나눠주기 (Distributing Handouts)

보충자료나 수준별 학습을 위한 학습지를 나눠주거나 다시 걷을 때 쓰는 표현이다. 학습지에 오류를 수정하거나 이미 나누어준 학습지를 학생들이 잘 관리하는지 확인한다.

#### Dialogue Practice ①

T: I have made two handouts on the subject.
Do you have the other two I gave you last class?
S: I don't know where I put them, sir. Do you have any extra?
T: You need to be more careful.
S: I am sorry, sir. I will clip them this time to my folder.
T: Now, are you going to lose them again?
S: No, sir. I will keep them secure.

#### Dialogue Practice ②

T: Here's a handout for today's lesson.
Please pass these back.
Did everyone get a handout?
S: No, I didn't.
T: Does anybody have an extra one?
S: I do. (hands the extra handout to teacher)
T: Thank you, Jin-Joo. (giving it to the other student) Here you are.

## Pattern Practice

1

| | | | | | |
|---|---|---|---|---|---|
| You'll need<br>Could you get out<br>Would you find | the materials<br>the sheets<br>the worksheets<br>the photocopies<br>the handouts<br>the passages | we<br>you | didn't finish<br>were using<br>had<br>began<br>handed round<br>gave out | last lesson<br>last week<br>last time | .(?) |

2

| | | | |
|---|---|---|---|
| Haven't you brought<br>Have you lost | yours? | Can you<br>You'll have to<br>You'd better | share with your neighbor? |

3

| | | | |
|---|---|---|---|
| I have some | papers<br>new books<br>worksheets | to pass out<br>to give out<br>to hand out | today. |

4

| | | |
|---|---|---|
| Please will you | give these out?<br>help your class captain? | Thanks. |

5

| | | | |
|---|---|---|---|
| Pass | these papers<br>this work | back<br>around<br>along | please. |

6

| | |
|---|---|
| Take one and pass them on.<br>Hand these papers around please. | They're for you to keep.<br>You may have them to keep. |

7

| | |
|---|---|
| I'm afraid you can't keep them.<br>I want these back please.<br>I want them back at the end of the lesson.<br>You must turn them in again so please don't write on them. | Alright?<br>OK? |

## Useful Expressions

| | |
|---|---|
| 학습지 나눠주기 | ■ Take one and pass them on.<br>■ Pass these out, please.<br>■ Pass around these handouts, please.<br>■ Pass these to the back.<br>■ Did everyone get a copy?<br>■ Here are handouts for this class. Please take care of them.<br>■ I will give you five handouts, so make sure you have all of them.<br>■ We are going to using these handouts over the next two months, so look after them.<br>■ I have several handouts for each of you. There are page numbers at the bottom. You arrange them accordingly.<br>■ Please staple the handouts, so that you can keep them all together.<br>■ Does everyone have the handout on 'to-infinitive'? |
| 학습지 걷기 | ■ I want to collect your work/assignments.<br>■ Please hand in your work/assignments.<br>■ Please pass your papers to the front.<br>■ Would you please collect the papers for me?<br>■ Hand in your papers as you leave.<br>■ Make sure your name is on your paper. |
| 학습지 오류 수정하기 | ■ I want to make a correction in the handout. Please look at page 1.<br>■ We have a poor printer. Would you write over the faint letters in the middle? |
| 학습지 관리하기 | ■ The handouts have run out.<br>■ I am short of handouts. Class president, please go get some for me.<br>■ I will be making some exam items out of this handout. Don't lose it.<br>■ I only have the originals, so I can't give you one. Please copy them yourself.<br>■ Do you have a stapler? I forgot to bring one. Can I borrow yours?<br>■ There is an extra margin on the left-hand side, so staple on the left side. |

## (2) OHP와 실물화상기 사용하기
## (Using an Overhead Projector and a Real Object Projector)

OHP나 실물 화상기, TV스크린 등을 이용하여 자료를 보여준다. 시각 수업을 하기 위해 교실 조명을 조절하고 시각 자료의 특정 부분에 주목하게 하며 시각 자료의 내용을 물어본다. 또한 자료가 선명하지 않을 때와 기계에 문제가 생겼을 때 OHP나 실물 화상기를 조작·관리하는 표현을 익혀둔다.

### Dialogue Practice ①

T: Mi-Jin, would you set up the overhead projector for me?

S: Yes, teacher. Shall I move it closer to the screen?

T: Let me see. Move it a little closer. More. O. K. That's good.

S: It doesn't work. The bulb is out.

T: It can't be. I used it last class. Did you plug it?

S: No, teacher. It's unplugged.

### Dialogue Practice ②

T: Which group wants to present their work?

Ss: Here. Here.

T: (pointing to group 3)
Group leader Hee-jin, will you come up here with your poster?

S: Yes, Miss Oh. (putting the poster on a real object projector)

T: Oh, the poster is tilted a little to the left. Would you straighten it?

S: Yes. (straightening the poster) How about now?

T: It's better now.

### Pattern Practice

1

| | | | |
|---|---|---|---|
| Could you | plug the | TV monitor<br>OHP<br>real object projector | in? |

2

| | |
|---|---|
| The socket is in<br>It plugs in | the wall near you. |

3

| | | |
|---|---|---|
| I'll turn it on. | It's | too bright.<br>not clear enough.<br>out of focus. |

4

| | | | |
|---|---|---|---|
| Please, | turn<br>put<br>switch | the lights<br>the overhead projector<br>the recorder | on<br>off. |

5

| | | |
|---|---|---|
| I'd better<br>I'll just | adjust the tone.<br>adjust the focus. | Is it better now? |

6

| | | | |
|---|---|---|---|
| What's wrong with it?<br>It doesn't work.<br>It doesn't seem to work.<br>I can't get it to work. | I'll just<br>Can you | check if the | plug is in.<br>switch is on.<br>main power (supply). |

7

| | | | | |
|---|---|---|---|---|
| The first | photo<br>image<br>thing<br>picture | I want to | show you<br>you to look at | is of a famous singer, Britney Spears.<br>was taken in Sydney.<br>is a good example of a typical American home.<br>will give you some idea of what high school life is like in UK.<br>will help you understand more about different housing in the world. |

8

| | | |
|---|---|---|
| In this one<br>in this picture | you can see | some typically English scenery.<br>a view from the Empire State Building.<br>a typical New York street scene. |

## Useful Expressions

| | |
|---|---|
| 전원 관리하기 | ■ Turn the lights on again.<br>■ Put the lights back on.<br>■ Pull the plug out.<br>■ Plug in the projector.<br>■ Unplug the projector.<br>■ Switch on the projector.<br>■ Lights out, please. |
| 도움 요청하기 | ■ Who is our projectionist today?<br>■ Who is going to change the slides?<br>■ Who would like to work the projector?<br>■ Who will operate the projector? |
| 커튼 내리고 올리기 | ■ Roll up the screen.<br>■ Put the screen away.<br>■ Draw the curtains.<br>■ Close the blinds.<br>■ Pull down the screen. |
| OHP, 실물화상기 관리하기 | ■ When you finish using it, keep the fan on to cool the OHP. Otherwise, the light bulbs will explode or the bulbs will burn out quickly.<br>■ The lens on the projector is dirty. Please clean it with tissue. Be careful not to scratch the surface.<br>■ When you move the OHP/real object projector, be careful. It is quite fragile and sensitive. Even a small bump may damage it.<br>■ When you put the transparency on the sensor, put the top part toward you.<br>■ Don't press on the optic sensor. It is breakable. Don't leave any finger prints on it, either.<br>■ Oh, the letters are smaller than I expected. I will make them larger.<br>■ When you fold the head part, don't press it too hard. You will break the neck. |
| 실물 화상기 조절하기 | ■ Adjust the focus, please.<br>■ A bit sharper, please.<br>■ I'm afraid this one is upside down/back to front.<br>■ I seem to have put this one in the wrong way round.<br>■ Let's put away this film. |

| | |
|---|---|
| 실물 화상기 조절하기 | ■ Hang on, I'll put it in again.<br>■ It's not clear enough. Something is wrong with the lens. Oh, I got it. It is dusty.<br>■ The image is reflected upside down.<br>■ Oh no! The picture is upside down. Turn it around.<br>■ The film is tilted a little to the right. Would you straighten it up? |
| 기계 오류 말하기 | ■ The projector doesn't seem to be working.<br>■ The bulb has gone/burnt out.<br>■ The slide cartridge seems to be stuck again.<br>■ Same old trouble again, I'm afraid.<br>■ The automatic focusing is not working.<br>■ It's out of focus. Let me adjust the head. O. K. now, it is a lot better.<br>■ It's not working. I'll have to go and ask Mr. Kim if he can fix it. |
| 시각 자료 제시하기 | ■ Let's look at some pictures.<br>■ I have a film to show you today.<br>■ I want you to look at this picture.<br>■ Tell me what's happening in the picture.<br>■ A map of London is shown on this screen.<br>■ This picture shows part of the British Museum.<br>■ I have some brochures about Wales.<br>■ This is an example of the Olympic Games.<br>■ In this picture, you can see some typical Beijing street scenes.<br>■ I'm going to show you some pictures of New Zealand.<br>■ There's a diagram I'd like to show you on the OHP. |
| 시각 자료에 대해 질문하기 | ■ Ask your friend some questions about it.<br>■ I'll ask you some questions about the picture.<br>■ What can you see in the picture?<br>■ Tell me what you can see.<br>■ What can you say about the picture?<br>■ What is there in the corner/ background?<br>■ What is happening in this picture?<br>■ Has anybody any idea what this (thing/ person) is called?<br>■ Do you notice anything odd/ strange/ unusual about this picture?<br>■ What time of day do you think it was taken? How can you tell?<br>■ In which season was this picture taken? How do you know?<br>■ By the way, could somebody read what it says on the notice.<br>■ Describe some of the people in the picture.<br>■ Can anybody point out the mistake in sentence 2? |

| | |
|---|---|
| 시각 자료에 대해 질문하기 | ■ Come and point out Beijing and Hong Kong for me.<br>■ Hyeonmin, will you put your recipe on the real object projector and explain how to make your Bibimbap?<br>■ Can anyone find any mistakes in the sentences on the screen?<br>■ Have you finished copying them? (No) O. K. I'll leave them on the board a little longer.<br>■ Would you overlap the second transparency on the first one? Now you can see changes in population growth.<br>■ Put the overhead closer to the screen. The image is larger than the screen can hold. |
| 사진이 선명하지 않을 때 사과하기 | ■ It's not awfully clear, I'm afraid.<br>■ It's not very sharp.<br>■ It's a bit out of focus.<br>■ I'm sorry about the colours.<br>■ There was probably something wrong with the film.<br>■ This one is rather underexposed/overexposed.<br>■ I was in a bit of a hurry when I look at this.<br>■ This was taken on a very cloudy day. |
| 특정 부분에 주의집중 유도하기 | ■ If you look carefully to the right of the shop, you'll see....<br>■ Can you make out the library, just to the left of the church?<br>■ See if you can pick out the shopkeeper.<br>■ Have a good/close look at the man standing in the boat.<br>■ Of particular interest in this picture is the costume.<br>■ Pay attention, especially to the way the girl is dancing.<br>■ Even if you look at nothing else, I think it's worth looking at... |
| 사진 속 인물이나 대상 가리키기 | ■ On the left/right.<br>■ On the far left/ left-hand side.<br>■ At the very edge of the picture.<br>■ At the top/ bottom.<br>■ In the top/ bottom left/ right-hand corner.<br>■ To the left of the white building.<br>■ Just a bit/ immediately to the right of the church.<br>■ In the (very) middle/center of the picture.<br>■ In the foreground/ background.<br>■ Just beyond the hill.<br>■ On the far/near bank of the river.<br>■ On the brow of the hill.<br>■ At the far end of the street. |

### (3) 녹음기, CD 플레이어, VCR 사용하기
### (Using a Cassette Tape Recorder, a CD Player or a VCR)

녹음기나 CD 플레이어, VCR를 이용하여 시청각 수업을 할 때, 음향과 화면을 조정하고, 시청각 자료를 제시한다. 수업 중 테이프나 CD, 비디오 등 기자재에 문제가 생겼을 때 필요한 표현들을 익혀두어 상황에 적절하게 대처한다.

#### Dialogue Practice ①

T: Today, you will have a listening and comprehension test.

S: We hate the test. It's quite frustrating.

T: I know how you feel. But, you can never improve your listening ability without practising listening.
The more you listen, the better you understand.

S: You can say that again, ma'am.

T: The material you are listening to is rather long and difficult, so pay attention.
Get set. Ready. Go!

#### Dialogue Practice ②

T: Let's watch a video now.
Can you see it all right?

Ss: Yes.

T: Good. How's the sound? Can you hear it clearly?

Ss: No.

T: (turning the sound up) How's that?

Ss: Good.

T: Now let's go back and watch it from the beginning.

## Pattern Practice

**1**

| | | | |
|---|---|---|---|
| Let me<br>Could you | plug<br>unplug | the tape recorder<br>the cassette player<br>the CD player<br>the video player<br>the radio | in.(?) |

**2**

| | |
|---|---|
| The socket is<br>The extension cord is | in the wall near you.<br>under the computer desk. |

**3**

| | | |
|---|---|---|
| I'd better<br>I'll just | turn the volume down.<br>turn it up a bit.<br>adjust the volume. | Is it better now?<br>Is it clear enough?<br>Can you hear it back there? |

**4**

<table>
<tr><td rowspan="2">It doesn't work.<br>It doesn't seem to work.<br>I can't get it to work.</td><td rowspan="2">I'll just<br>Let me<br>Can you</td><td>check if the</td><td>plug is in<br>switch is on<br>main power supply stays on</td><td rowspan="2">.(?)</td></tr>
<tr><td colspan="2">unplug it<br>take the plug out<br>switch it off at the wall</td></tr>
</table>

## Useful Expressions

### A. 녹음기, CD 플레이어 이용하기 (Using a tape recorder, and CD player)

| | |
|---|---|
| 테이프나<br>CD 듣기 | ■ Let's listen to the tape/CD now.<br>■ First of all, listen to the conversation.<br>■ Now you'll hear the sentences on the tape/CD.<br>■ What you will hear is a conversation.<br>■ Here it goes.<br>■ Off we go then.<br>■ Here it comes.<br>■ Don't talk with your partner, just listen.<br>■ Just listen. Don't say anything.<br>■ Listen carefully to the instructions. |

| | |
|---|---|
| 테이프나 CD 듣기 | ■ Listen but don't write anything.<br>■ Make sure you concentrate on the contents of the tape/CD.<br>■ As you listen, do exercise 5.<br>■ As you listen, fill in the missing words.<br>■ While you listen/ you are listening, answer question 2.<br>■ While listening, mark your answer sheet.<br>■ Before listening, read through the questions.<br>■ Before listening again, familiarize yourselves with the questions.<br>■ The script for the listening material is on the back of your book. |
| 노래 들려주기 | ■ Now I have a song for you.<br>■ Listen to the words of the song.<br>■ Try to follow what the singer is saying.<br>■ Here's a song by Sweet Box called 'Life is cool.' |
| 다시 듣기 | ■ Let's listen to it once more/ one more time.<br>■ Now we'll listen to it again.<br>■ We have enough time to listen to it again.<br>■ We'll stop here/there for a moment.<br>■ Before we go on, I'll ask some questions.<br>■ We'll go back and listen again. Ready?<br>■ I'll let you hear it again before I ask you these questions.<br>■ I'll play the tape/CD twice and then you reconstruct the contents for yourself, OK?<br>■ I will give you a dictation test. You write down what you hear from the tape. |
| 소리 조절하기 | ■ Can you all hear?<br>■ Is it clear enough?<br>■ Is the sound clear enough?<br>■ Can everybody hear?<br>■ Is the volume all right?<br>■ Can you hear me at the back?<br>■ Is there anybody who can't hear me?<br>■ Is there anybody having trouble?<br>■ I'll adjust the volume.<br>■ I'll turn the volume up/down.<br>■ I am adjusting the volume. Can you hear it in the back? |

| | |
|---|---|
| 소리 조절하기 | ■ This is full volume.<br>■ This is the maximum. I can't make it louder. Sorry.<br>■ If you can't hear, come a bit nearer.<br>■ Is that better?<br>■ I've got too much treble and not enough bass. |
| 테이프나 CD에 문제가 생겼을 때 | ■ The tape recorder/CD player seems to be broken.<br>■ There seems to be something wrong (with it).<br>■ The CD player isn't working properly.<br>■ Do any of you know anything about the CD player?<br>■ The tape is chewed up.<br>■ This tape has loosened so it sounds terrible.<br>■ Just a minute. I can't find the exact spot.<br>■ I seem to have brought the wrong tape.<br>■ We'll have to do something else, I'm afraid.<br>■ Oh. It's the wrong side. Let me take it out and turn it over.<br>■ I put the wrong tape/CD in. I am sorry. I will go and get the right one.<br>■ I'll find the place.<br>■ Wait a moment/second/minute. I'll just rewind the tape.<br>■ Let me just find the beginning again.<br>■ Look at the questions while I find the place.<br>■ I'm afraid I played the wrong track. Let me find the right one.<br>■ Today's material is far ahead. Let me press the "fast forward" button.<br>■ The tape recorder runs a little fast, so the sound sounds awkward. I think we should adjust the speed. |

## B. 비디오 이용하기 (Using a VCR)

| | |
|---|---|
| 비디오 보여주기 | ■ Let's watch this video.<br>■ We're going to watch a video.<br>■ Why don't we watch a video now?<br>■ Let me turn this knob, the volume control.<br>■ Draw the curtain so that you can see the screen clearly.<br>■ Can you hear at the back? |

| | |
|---|---|
| 비디오 보여주기 | ■ Can you see the screen well at the back?<br>■ In this class, you will watch the movie, "Hair Spray."<br>■ Did you understand? Let me go back and play it again.<br>■ Now we'll watch the video without the sound.<br>■ Let's watch it without the sound.<br>■ Pay attention to the scene where they are talking about the solar system.<br>■ After watching the movie, you'll have to write your movie review in English.<br>■ Try to listen to what they say, instead of just watching the movie.<br>■ While watching the videos, write down what you hear.<br>■ You can buy a video tape with English subtitles. At first, try not to read the captions. Instead, listen to what they say again and again.<br>■ If the video tape has subtitles, you hide them with a strip of paper. After watching it once or twice, you remove the strip and check the parts you couldn't understand.<br>■ There are always some parts which you can never understand what they say. In this case, ask for help from your teacher or you can read the subtitles.<br>■ Some videos are good, but some are bad for you. They are x-rated.<br>* G (General Audiences): 일반용<br>* PG (Parental Guidance): 보호자의 지도 필요<br>* PG-13: 부모의 강력한 주의가 요망, 13세 미만의 어린이들에게는 부적절할 수도 있음<br>* R (Restricted): 17세 이하는 부모나 성인보호자 동반시 관람 가<br>* NC-17 (No Children-17 or older) / X: 17세 이하 미성년자 관람 불가<br>* NR / No rated: 등급 없음 |
| 비디오에 문제가 생겼을 때 | ■ It's not loud enough.<br>■ Is the picture clear?<br>■ Let's find the right place on the tape.<br>■ It's too loud. I need to adjust the volume.<br>■ The picture is not clear. I need to adjust it. |

### (4) 컴퓨터 이용하기 (Using a Computer)

컴퓨터 전원 켜고 끄기와 파일 저장하기, CD/DVD 사용하기, 인터넷 연결하기와 같은 컴퓨터와 관련된 일반적인 표현과 수업 중 컴퓨터가 다운되거나 바이러스에 감염됐을 때에 대처하는 표현을 알아둔다. 인터넷 검색을 통해 원하는 정보를 검색한 후 자료를 저장하고 편집하거나, 전 세계의 온라인 박물관, 유적지, 도서관 등을 방문하여 사회문화적 다양성을 인식하고 다양한 정보를 습득한다.

#### Dialogue Practice ①

S: Oh, my gosh. All of a sudden, my keyboard is frozen.

T: Did you save what you've been working on?

S: Fortunately, I did.

T: That's a relief. What's wrong with the computer, by the way?

S: I have no idea. Can I move to the next computer? I think I should keep working on it and print it out.

T: Sure, why not? Please check to see if the computer is connected to the printer.

S: Okay, I will.

#### Dialogue Practice ②

T: Last time, we learned the song, "With You" by Chris Brown.
Do you like the song?

S: Yes!

T: Today, you can watch the music video of that song.

S: Wow!

T: I'll show you how to access it. First, type utube.com in the address box. Then you can see the website. Type "With You" on the search box. There are many music videos for that song. Click the one you want. If you want full screen, click the icon on the bottom right. Are you following me?

S: Yes, we can see it too.

## A. 컴퓨터 사용하기 (Using a Computer)

### Pattern Practice

1

| Let me<br>Let's<br>I'll | turn<br>switch<br>log | the computer<br>the PC | on.<br>off. |
|---|---|---|---|

2

| Are you | connected to<br>on | the Internet? |
|---|---|---|
| Do you<br>Can you | have access to<br>access<br>get on | |

3

| Do you know<br>Can you tell me<br>Who knows | how to | connect a printer to the computer<br>move and click on the mouse<br>download a program<br>load a program<br>compile data<br>make a backup copy of your file<br>save your data<br>install this program in the computer<br>scan a picture<br>chat on the computer<br>insert and remove a USB cable<br>work on Photoshop | ? |
|---|---|---|---|

### Useful Expressions

| 컴퓨터 전원 켜고 끄기 | ▪ Please type in the password.<br>▪ Remove (Take out) the disk.<br>▪ Turn on the computer, please.<br>▪ Turn off the computer, please.<br>▪ Switch on the computer, please.<br>▪ Let's switch off the computer.<br>▪ Will you log on the computer?<br>▪ Why don't you log off the computer? |
|---|---|

| | |
|---|---|
| 파일 저장하기 | ■ Now, clip this news article. Go to the word processor, open a new file and paste it. Now you can save it as a new name.<br>■ Store this file on the C drive.<br>■ Click the file and drag it into A folder/ USB.<br>■ There is not a lot of memory in the D drive.<br>■ What is the memory of the computer?<br>■ Are you sure you inserted the disk/USB?<br>■ Let's insert a USB into the computer. Open your folder and save the document. |
| 컴퓨터로 CD나 DVD 사용하기 | ■ Let's watch a clip from the CD-ROM/DVD.<br>■ Look at the screen, please.<br>■ Insert your CDs into your CD-ROM drive.<br>■ Take out your CDs from your CD-ROM drive.<br>■ You can play your CDs/DVDs using players like window media player or Gom player.<br>■ You can choose subtitles by clicking each language type.<br>■ If you do not want to see subtitles, choose "no subtitle".<br>■ Last class we watched the scene with the seven dwarfs. Do you want to continue the story or review from the beginning?<br>■ If you want to copy this movie, you can use a CD writing program on the Internet.<br>■ Download CD writing programs from freeware web sites.<br>■ Insert an empty CD into E drive and follow instructions. |
| 인터넷 연결하기 | ■ Is this computer connected on to the Internet?<br>■ This is the Internet Explorer icon. It is the browser which makes you go into cyberspace.<br>■ Connect/log on to an online service/ to the Internet.<br>■ First move the mouse and point to the Internet Explorer icon and click twice(=double-click).<br>■ These icons represent their software programs.<br>■ When you click on one of them, it starts to work. |
| | ■ Go onto the Internet.<br>■ Get onto the Internet.<br>■ Explore the Internet. |

**인터넷 이용하여 자료 찾기**

- Surf the Internet.
- Browse the Internet.
- Visit the Web site of the New York Times. Read news headlines and write down three headlines from America and the world.
- Do you know the names of search engines? Some of them are Google, Daum, Naver, and Nate.
- Make groups of five or six students. Each student visits one of the search engines.
- When you use Google, you just write your topic or word(s) such as 'American Museums' in the search box. And then hit enter, you can get a new page filled with the results. Just take a look at the categories and choose one to click on.
- Did you find what you were looking for?
- Compare your results with those of others.
- Now visit one of the American museums on the Net.
- Why don't you add this to your bookmark?
- Find sites which tell you what costumes are popular among children.
- Compare your search at one search engine with those of your friends'. Are they similar or not?
- Go to the sites concerning costumes and find out what costumes are available.
- Find sites which cover July 4th traditions.
- There are many good Web sites to satisfy any movie fan.
- You can go to the Kungfu Panda's official site at www.kungfupanda.com and see the trailer.
- Did you see the trailer for "the Golden Compass" on the Net?
- Which sites have a lot of information on Martin Luther King's achievements in civil rights?
- Which sites offer audio version of his speeches?
- Summarize the information you have in English or in Korean.
- Although it takes about ten minutes to download the trailer, it's worth the time.
- Don't chat on the computer during the class.

| 컴퓨터와 관련된 일반적인 표현 | ■ This is the starting screen.<br>■ Now, change the background screen pattern into 'the sea bottom'.<br>■ Shall I print it out for you?<br>■ How many words can you type in a minute?<br>■ Did you type the entire report?<br>■ I edited it using Microsoft Word.<br>■ Just change the date on the computer.<br>■ The speed of this computer is slowing down.<br>■ Our school has LAN or local area network and all the computers are connected to the school main computer. |
|---|---|

## B. 컴퓨터 문제해결하기 (Solving a Computer Problem)

### Pattern Practice

**4**

| | |
|---|---|
| The computer<br>The screen | is frozen.<br>crashed<br>is down.<br>is out of order.<br>needs to be fixed. |

**5**

| | | | |
|---|---|---|---|
| The<br>A | keyboard<br>speaker<br>drive | doesn't<br>doesn't seem to | work. |
| | | isn't | working. |
| | | is | broken. |

**6**

| | | | | |
|---|---|---|---|---|
| The computer | has a<br>got a | problem.<br>virus.<br>malicious code. | It's | the "Friday the 13th" virus.<br>a "Trojan horse" virus. |

### Useful Expressions

| | |
|---|---|
| 컴퓨터 문제 알리기 | ■ I have a systems failure.<br>■ My computer's down again.<br>■ The computer control started blinking.<br>■ I erased all the data by mistake.<br>■ This computer isn't connected to the printer.<br>■ Oh, why does the "error" sign keep appearing?<br>■ It's taking a long time to download the file.<br>■ Oh my goodness! I haven't saved(backed up) my work yet and it's down again.<br>■ Computers are beyond me. |
| 컴퓨터 바이러스 감염 표현하기 | ■ I think your system caught a virus.<br>■ Some viruses destroy all files.<br>■ The computer has a virus / got a virus.<br>■ I can't get rid of the virus / remove the virus.<br>■ Download the vaccine program at www.ahnlab.com.<br>■ Today is "Friday the 13th". The computer might get the "Friday the 13th" virus.<br>■ Before opening a file, please check to see if it has any computer viruses. |

## 4) 학생 관리하기 (Classroom Management)

### (1) 학생 통제하기 (Controlling Students)

교사의 수업 진행을 위해 학생들의 주의집중이 필요할 때 쓰는 표현이다. 수업에 방해가 되는 학생들의 잡담, 휴대폰 사용을 금지시키며 자세나 말투를 교정하기 주의, 경고를 한다.

### Dialogue Practice ①

T: Class, stop what you are doing and pay attention to me, please.

S: But we haven't finished our pair work yet.

T: I know, but that's O. K. Please get on with your work quietly. Put your desks back where they were.

Ss: Yes, teacher.

T: Dong-Ho, stop moving around. Go back to your seat, please.

D: Sorry, sir. I'll go back.

## Dialogue Practice ②

T: Min-Seok, can you translate this sentence into Korean?

S: I don't know.

T: Come on, I know you can do it.

S: I don't know.

T: OK, here's a tip. Look at this card first and try once more.

S: I said I don't know.

T: Min-Seok, if you keep saying I don't know and never try as you do now, I will have to give you the lowest grade.

S: Whatever.

T: What did you just say?

S: I didn't say anything.

T: I can hear you and I can't stand it any more. Come see me in detention after school.

## Pattern Practice

**1**

<table>
<tr><td>No</td><td>talking<br>writing</td><td rowspan="2">while</td><td rowspan="2">I'm talking.<br>I'm writing on the blackboard.<br>I'm explaining this.<br>we're doing this.<br>the others are still working.</td></tr>
<tr><td rowspan="2">Don't</td><td>talk<br>write</td></tr>
<tr><td colspan="2">talk with your parter while you're</td><td>listening to me.<br>reading books.<br>solving questions.</td></tr>
</table>

**2**

<table>
<tr><td>Don't<br>You mustn't<br>You'd better not</td><td>talk<br>start<br>answer<br>write it down<br>read it<br>write it</td><td>until<br>unless</td><td>I tell you to.<br>I've finished.<br>I let you.<br>you've understood.<br>I ask you to.<br>I've said it all.<br>everyone's ready.<br>everyone's finished.</td></tr>
<tr><td>You needn't</td><td>translate</td><td>unless</td><td>I ask you to.</td></tr>
</table>

**3**

<table>
<tr><td rowspan="2">Wait a minute!</td><td rowspan="2">Not<br>No, not</td><td rowspan="2">this<br>that</td><td>one.<br>book.<br>card.<br>page.<br>picture.<br>exercise.<br>dialogue.</td><td>This</td><td>one.<br>book.<br>card.<br>page.<br>picture.<br>exercise.<br>dialogue.</td><td>Here.</td></tr>
<tr><td>way.</td><td>This</td><td>way.</td><td>Like this.</td></tr>
</table>

**4**

<table>
<tr><td>You've</td><td>brought<br>done<br>got</td><td rowspan="2">the<br>wrong</td><td rowspan="2">book,<br>page,<br>exercise,<br>one,</td><td>haven't you?</td><td rowspan="3">What did I tell you to do?<br>Who can remember what I said?</td></tr>
<tr><td rowspan="2">You're</td><td>reading<br>doing</td><td rowspan="2">aren't you?</td></tr>
<tr><td colspan="3">doing it in the wrong way.</td></tr>
</table>

**5**

<table>
<tr><td rowspan="2">Could you</td><td>do it</td><td>how<br>the way</td><td rowspan="2">I told you to?<br>I asked you to?</td></tr>
<tr><td>read<br>write</td><td>the bit<br>the exercise</td></tr>
</table>

**6**

<table>
<tr><td>Will you</td><td>be quiet,<br>watch out,<br>try harder,<br>be careful,</td><td>please?</td></tr>
</table>

**7**

| If you don't | pay attention,<br>listen properly,<br>concentrate, | it'll go in one ear and out the other. |
|---|---|---|

## Useful Expressions

| | |
|---|---|
| 주의 집중시키기 | ■ Look at me.<br>■ Look this way.<br>■ Face the front.<br>■ Pay attention now.<br>■ Try to concentrate now.<br>■ Eyes to the front, please.<br>■ Don't look out the window.<br>■ Don't sit there daydreaming.<br>■ Could I have your attention, please? |
| 잡담 금지시키기 | ■ Silence, please.<br>■ Get on with it, please.<br>■ Please be quiet!<br>■ Stop chatting there.<br>■ What is all the commotion about? Please pay attention.<br>■ What's all this noise?<br>■ Listen to what I'm saying.<br>■ Get on with your work quietly.<br>■ Don't bang the top of your desks.<br>■ Could I have a bit of quiet, please?<br>※ Shut up, all of you. – 교실상황에서는 부적절한 표현 |
| 바른 자세로 앉게 하기 | ■ Turn this way.<br>■ Stop fidgeting.<br>■ Stand (Sit) still.<br>■ Nobody moves.<br>■ Behave yourself.<br>■ Sit up (straight).<br>■ Stay in your seat.<br>■ I need you to act more mature.<br>■ No, that's not the way to do pair practice.<br>■ Now then that's not the way to behave in class. |

| | |
|---|---|
| 바른 자세로 앉게 하기 | ■ No writing while I'm writing on the blackboard.<br>■ Would you please straighten the chairs? Sit upright. Look at me. Eyes front. Are you ready? Today's lesson is about how to make friends. |
| 말투 교정시키기 | ■ Softer.<br>■ Speak up.<br>■ Say it once more.<br>■ Speak more clearly.<br>■ Once again, but louder.<br>■ Use a complete sentence.<br>■ There's no need to shout.<br>■ The whole sentence, please.<br>■ Say after me, "He has gone."<br>■ Once again, but more clearly.<br>■ Again, but more quickly this time.<br>■ Repeat after me, "It's a blue car."<br>■ Say it so that everyone can hear you. |
| 버릇없는 학생 주의주기 | ■ Would you take the snack off your desk? You are not watching the TV show.<br>■ You are reading cartoons during the class. Why? Is this class boring?<br>■ Hey, you are still chewing gum? That is not allowed during class.<br>■ Spit it out right away. (Remove it right away. Take it out.)<br>■ Don't talk with your friends while I am explaining. Other students can't hear what I say.<br>■ Be quiet, and pay attention to what Ji-Yeon is saying. I will ask some questions later.<br>■ It is rude to chat when someone is explaining.<br>■ Behave yourself, guys. You are not children anymore.<br>■ Please don't talk when someone else is talking. You should know better than that.<br>■ You can choose whether you listen to me or not. But I can't stand your disturbing the class and bothering other students.<br>■ If you don't act like students, you will be treated as such. Be nice! How you will be treated depends on what you do.<br>■ Don't you know what to do and what not to do? You should know better, girls! If you are a student, be like one. What you do doesn't become a student. |

## (2) 학생 훈육하기 (Disciplining Students)

학생들이 수업시간에 지켜야할 규정을 위반한 것에 대해서 교사가 주의를 주었음에도 불구하고 같은 행동을 반복했을 때 이를 처리하는 방법으로 경고, 신체적 벌, 압수, 청소를 시키는 방법이 있다. 경고의 유형에는 학생/교사 또는 부모/교사와의 상담, 반성문 쓰기, 교칙에 의한 처벌 등이 있다. 이외에도 신체적 벌을 주거나 만화책, 휴대폰, 악세서리와 같은 물품의 압수, 교내 청소 등이 학생을 훈육하기 위한 방법으로 사용된다.

### Dialogue Practice ①

T: Ji-Min, stand up, please.

S: Yes, Mr. Kim.

T: You're so noisy that I cannot continue my lesson.

S: I'm so sorry.

T: Stand in the back of the classroom for the rest of this class.

S: Please give me a break, sir. I won't be noisy any more.

### Dialogue Practice ②

T: Is that a cell-phone? Whose is it?

S: It's mine, Miss Kim. I'm really sorry. I forgot to turn it off.

T: No cell-phone in school. You know the rule, don't you?

S: Please, Miss Kim.
My homeroom teacher will call my parents if you take it.
So please give me a break.

T: The rule is the rule. Give it to me.

S: Teacher, please.

## Pattern Practice

1

| | | | |
|---|---|---|---|
| If you | do that once more,<br>forget it one more time,<br>don't work harder,<br>keep on wasting time,<br>don't do your homework again, | I'll<br>I'll have to<br>I'll definitely | punish you.<br>send you to your homeroom teacher.<br>tell your parents.<br>write to your parents. |

2

| | |
|---|---|
| No, don't do that!<br>Stop it.<br>That's enough.<br>You're doing the same thing over and over. | I can't stand it any more. |

3

| | | |
|---|---|---|
| Stand up and | go to the hallway<br>stretch your arms forward<br>go to the back of the classroom<br>come to the front of the classroom | for the rest of the class. |

4

| | | | |
|---|---|---|---|
| You're using your | cell-phone<br>MP3 player<br>PSP | in the class. | I have to take it from you.<br>Give it to me. |

## Useful Expressions

### A. 경고하기 (Warning)

| | |
|---|---|
| 부모와 상담 경고하기 | ■ I think I need to counsel with your parents.<br>■ It has nothing to do with you. I will call your parents and talk with them. |
| 교사와 상담 경고하기 | ■ Min-Su, come to the teacher's room after the class.<br>■ If you keep that disrespectful attitude toward the teachers, you will be sent to the Dean of Students' Affairs. He will teach you how to behave.<br>■ I don't want to see the two of you to sit together again. You are more interested in chatting. If you keep misbehaving, I will ask your homeroom teacher to take care of you. |

| | |
|---|---|
| 반성문 작성 경고하기 | ■ What you said was quite insulting. How dare you use such bad language in front of me? Write a letter of apology. |
| 교칙에 의한 처벌 경고하기 | ■ If you keep doing wrong, I will have to take necessary steps to discipline you.<br>■ If you still don't regret what you have done, you will be treated according to school regulations.<br>■ How are you doing, Da-Eun? I see you have dyed your hair. You know it is against school regulations. Unless you go back to your natural color, I will put your name on a demerit system card.<br>■ Do you know the demerit system? If you misbehave during the class, I will keep a record of your misbehavior. |
| 상황에 따른 처벌 경고하기 | ■ You're late again. I won't let you come in the classroom next time.<br>■ Your class wasn't good in the last exam. To make you study harder, I'll check your notebooks everyday to know whether you concentrate on the class or not. |

## B. 신체적 벌 (Corporal Punishment)

| | |
|---|---|
| 체벌하기 | ■ Do 20 push-ups.<br>■ Get down on your knees!<br>■ Go to the back and raise your hands until I tell you not to.<br>■ You're so noisy. Go back to the classroom and stand still.<br>■ Stand up with your eyes closed.<br>■ You go out and stand in the hallway.<br>■ If you keep talking during class, I will put you at the corner of the classroom alone.<br>■ You have been told to be quiet several times, but still make noise. Stretch your arms forward and keep that position for 3 minutes. If your arms go down, I will add two more minutes. |

## C. 압수 (Confiscation)

| | |
|---|---|
| 금지 물품 압수하기 | ■ You're not supposed to read comic books in class. Give it to me. I will not return it.<br>■ Using a cell phone is not allowed in the class. I have to take it from you. Come to the teacher's room after class.<br>■ You shouldn't wear earrings in school. Give them/it to me right now. You will be given them/it a month later. |

## D. 청소시키기 (Cleaning punishment)

| | |
|---|---|
| 청소시키기 | ■ Clean up all the windows as a penalty for cheating. You should feel grateful that the punishment is light.<br>■ You didn't do your homework so you should stay at/after school till you finish the work.<br>■ Please come to school early and clean up the classroom to make up for the trouble you caused.<br>■ Please make a list of new words in the previous test and memorize them by writing them down on paper. If you fail to do this, you will clean up the rest rooms. |

## 3. 수업 정리 (Consolidation)

### 1) 형성평가 (Formative Test)

수업 후 학습 내용 이해를 확인하기 위해 학습지를 나눠주고 각 문항별로 정답과 오답률을 환산하여 수업의 효율성 내지 학습자의 학습 결함 여부를 확인한다. 형성 평가를 통해 학습자가 학습 내용을 이해하고 있는지 확인하고 곤란을 겪고 있거나 학습 결함을 보인 경우 학습 목표를 학습자의 수준에 맞게 조정하고 학습 내용을 보다 쉽게 구성하는 등 교수-학습의 방법을 바꾸도록 한다.

#### Dialogue Practice ①

T: We have only 5 minutes now. I want to know if you understand today's lesson well. Pass these worksheets around and answer the questions on it. I'll give you 3 minutes. This is just a formative test, so no cheating, Ok?

Ss: (pass the test around and solve it) Yes.

T: Time is over. Are you finished? Put your pens down.

Ss: Yes.

T: Let's check the answers together.

#### Dialogue Practice ②

T: Let me see how much you've learned today. We're going to take a check up test now. Listen, you should try these three questions. Try to answer by yourselves. (after a few minutes) Are you done?

S: No, I'm not.

T: Hurry up. Now, let's check the answers.

## Pattern Practice

1

| | |
|---|---|
| I'll give you<br>You can have<br>You can take | five more minutes. |

2

| | | |
|---|---|---|
| Would you<br>How'd you like to | read the directions? | |
| Will you | read the directions,<br>Read the directions, | for us?<br>please.(would you?) |

3

| | | | |
|---|---|---|---|
| Raise your hand | if<br>when<br>in case | you | have any questions.<br>need some help.<br>are having trouble. |

4

| | | |
|---|---|---|
| Let's | check<br>look at<br>go over | the answer.(together) |

5

| | |
|---|---|
| Why did<br>Can you tell us why<br>Can you explain why | you choose B? |

6

| | | |
|---|---|---|
| What did you | get<br>say<br>put(down) | for question two? |

7

| | | |
|---|---|---|
| Let's | see how you did with<br>see what you did with | question number three.<br>question three. |

## Useful Expressions

| | |
|---|---|
| 학습지 나누기 | ■ Close your books.<br>■ Take one sheet.<br>■ Pass them around.<br>■ Please share the handout with your partner. |
| 지시하기 | ■ Do exercise 5. = Try exercise 5.<br>■ No cheating.<br>■ Make sure your name is on your paper.<br>■ Do the whole activity.<br>■ If you get stuck, skip the question.<br>■ If you get stuck on one, leave it out and come back to it later. |
| 시간 제한하기 | ■ I'll give you 10 minutes. = You have 10 minutes.<br>■ Are you almost done?<br>■ Are you finished?<br>■ Please hurry up.<br>■ Do you need more time?<br>■ I'll give you five more minutes.<br>■ Time's up. = It's time to stop. = We're out of time.<br>■ Put your pencil down. = Pens down everyone. |
| 정답 확인하기 | ■ Let's check the answers.<br>■ Check your answers on page 35.<br>■ Mark your own.<br>■ What's the correct answer to question 1?<br>= What do you have for question 1?<br>■ What do you have for question 2?<br>■ The answers are on page 125.<br>= Check the answers on page 125.<br>■ Is everything clear?<br>■ Do you understand everything? |
| 짝과 바꾸기 | ■ Exchange papers with your partners.<br>■ Change papers with a friend. |
| 점수 확인 | ■ Count up your points.<br>■ Take off one point for every one wrong.<br>■ How many answers did you get right?<br>■ How many did you get wrong?<br>■ What was your score? |

| | |
|---|---|
| 점수 확인 | ■ How many points did you score?<br>■ Did anyone get them all right?<br>■ Is there anybody with one/two mistake(s)? |
| 학습지 걷기 | ■ Please pass your papers to the front.<br>■ Hand in your papers as you leave. |

## 2) 피드백 (Feedback)

교수-학습 과정의 각 단계에서 학생에게 피드백을 준다. 학생들이 수업 도중 실수하거나 잘못된 답을 말했을 때 적절하게 교정해주고 보충할 기회를 제공함으로써 오류가 화석화되는 것을 막고 학습 결손의 누적 현상을 피한다. 피드백을 통해 학습자 스스로 틀린 원인을 발견하고 수정하면서 과제를 성공적으로 수행할 수 있도록 한다.

### Dialogue Practice ①

T: Today, we will learn the words about various jobs. Look at the picture on the screen, and tell me what the people do for their living. First, what is this man's job?

Ss: Photo.

T: Well, photo is not a name of job. But, taking a photo is his job. Think again and tell me the correct answer.

S: Photographer.

T: Good job. He is a photographer.
Look at the second picture. What is the woman's occupation?

S: Talent.

T: Good try, but talent is not a correct answer. It is even not a proper English expression in this situation. Talent as a TV star is a Konglish expression.

S: Actor.

T: Much better. But you've forgotten something here. This person is a woman, not a man.

S: Actress?

T: Correct!

## Dialogue Practice ②

T: Good morning everyone. Nice Monday morning, isn't it?

S: Yes.

T: Hey, Hee-Jin, you look so tired. What's up?

S: I did so many things yesterday.

T: Oh, really? What did you do?

S: I go to my grandparent's house with my father and mother.

T: Yesterday, not today? Right?

S: Yes.

T: Then, check your grammar. There is something wrong.

S: Oh, I know what it is.
I went to my grandparent's house.

T: You got it.

## Pattern Practice

**1**

<table><tr><td rowspan="2">That's</td><td rowspan="2">quite good,<br>much better,<br>very neat,</td><td rowspan="2">but</td><td colspan="2">what's wrong<br>there's something wrong</td><td>in this</td><td>line<br>word<br>phrase<br>text</td><td>?</td></tr><tr><td>you've</td><td colspan="2">forgotten something<br>left something out</td><td colspan="2">here.</td></tr></table>

**2**

<table><tr><td>Check<br>It's<br>What about</td><td>your</td><td>spelling of '________'<br>punctuation<br>handwriting<br>grammar<br>capital letters</td><td>. (?)</td></tr></table>

**3**

<table>
<tr><td rowspan="5">Good try,<br>Good guess,</td><td rowspan="5">but</td><td>are these</td><td rowspan="2">alright<br>right<br>correct</td><td rowspan="5">?</td></tr>
<tr><td>is this</td></tr>
<tr><td colspan="2">have you done this alright</td></tr>
<tr><td>is this</td><td>what you want<br>how you mean</td></tr>
<tr><td colspan="2">do you think it is right?<br>Can you find any mistakes here</td></tr>
</table>

**4**

<table>
<tr><td>Is that a</td><td>true<br>good</td><td>sentence?<br>answer?</td><td rowspan="2">Can you read it to me?<br>Could you read what you have written please?<br>Does it make sense, or is it silly?<br>What do you have to do?</td></tr>
<tr><td colspan="3">What do you all think?<br>Think what that means!</td></tr>
</table>

## Useful Expressions

| | |
|---|---|
| 실수 지적하기 | ■ It's close.<br>■ Try again.<br>■ Think again.<br>■ Will you try it again?<br>■ Good try, but you're not quite right.<br>■ (That's) Almost right but not correct.<br>■ Good try but you're not quite right. |
| 오답 수정하기 | ■ You forgot the preposition.<br>■ Check the grammar/tense/number agreement.<br>■ Think about the grammar/tense/number agreement. |
| 격려하기 | ■ That's much better.<br>■ Go on, and have a try.<br>■ Don't worry about it.<br>■ You're getting better at it all the time.<br>■ You've made a lot of progress.<br>■ I believe you can do better next time. |

### 3) 칭찬하기 (Compliments)

학생들이 수업 시간에 적극적으로 참여하고 올바른 영어를 발화하였을 때, 칭찬해주고 더 잘할 수 있도록 격려해 주는 영어 표현이다. 칭찬과 격려를 통해 학습 내용에 자신감과 만족감을 갖고, 학습자의 내적 동기를 유발하여 적극적으로 차후의 학습 단원에 임할 수 있도록 한다.

#### Dialogue Practice ①

T: I told you to make an English poster. Are you all done?

Ss: Yes.

T: Great. Let's take a look at your work.
Who would like to go first?

S: I'd like to show mine, teacher.

T: OK. Han-Seok, come up here and show yours to the class.

S: (shows his poster to the class)

T: Wonderful! Everyone, let's give a big hand to him and say good job.

Ss: Good job.

#### Dialogue Practice ②

T: First, listen carefully to the dialogue and then answer the question. (switches on the dialogue.) Where did In-Su go during vacation?

Ss: He visited his friend in New York.

T: Very good. Si-Young, what did he do in New York?

Si-Young: He went sightseeing.

T: Excellent! Where did he go?

Si-Young: He went to the Empire State Building and the Statue of Liberty.

T: Exactly. You did a very good listening. What else did he do? Does anybody have the answer? Yes, Su-Jin, what did he do after he visited the Empire State Building and the Statue of Liberty?

Su-Jin: He saw a broadway show.

T: That's perfect. Then, let's move on to the next section. I will show you nice pictures of New York. Let's trace back where In-Su and his friend visited.

## Pattern Practice

**1**

<table>
<tr><td rowspan="3">That's</td><td>it.<br>quite right.<br>correct.<br>the way.</td></tr>
<tr><td>very good.<br>nice.<br>very cool.</td></tr>
<tr><td>a very good point.<br>perfectly correct.<br>exactly the point.<br>just what I was looking for.<br>very thoughtful of you.<br>so honest of you.</td></tr>
</table>

**2**

<table>
<tr><td rowspan="2">You</td><td>are</td><td>right.<br>so clever.<br>very brilliant.</td></tr>
<tr><td colspan="2">did a very good job.<br>did such a wonderful(excellent) work.<br>made a very good job of that.<br>didn't make a single mistake.<br>worked really hard today.<br>have become a better reader(listener, writer, speaker).</td></tr>
<tr><td>You've</td><td colspan="2">got the idea.<br>got it.</td></tr>
</table>

**3**

<table>
<tr><td>Your</td><td>pronunciation<br>writing<br>summary<br>guess<br>role play<br>conversation</td><td>is very good.</td></tr>
</table>

## Useful Expressions

| | |
|---|---|
| 학생의 정답 확인해주기 | ■ That's right.<br>■ You got the correct answer.<br>■ Yes, the answer is ~. |
| 칭찬하기 | ■ That couldn't be better.<br>■ I have high hopes for you.<br>■ I really like the way that you speak.<br>■ There's nothing wrong with your answer.<br>■ You read it very nicely.<br>■ I'm so proud of you.<br>■ You're very clever.<br>■ That's a good example.<br>■ Your pronunciation is very good.<br>■ I'm sure you can do well.<br>■ I see many people who did/are doing the right thing.<br>■ I couldn't have given a better answer myself. |
| 간단한 칭찬 표현 사용하기 | ■ Very fascinating.<br>■ Great work today!<br>■ Sounds wonderful.<br>■ Right you are.<br>■ That's perfect.<br>■ Very well done.<br>■ You did well.<br>■ Marvellous.<br>■ Super nice.<br>■ Good stuff.<br>■ Very interesting.<br>■ Great improvement.<br>■ Excellent work.<br>■ Perfect! Keep it up.<br>■ That's almost right.<br>■ OK. You've got it. |
| 다른 학생의 칭찬 유도하기 | ■ Cheer for him.<br>■ Let's give him a big hand.<br>■ Let's give him a big round of applause. |

## 4) 숙제 내주기 (Assignments)

수업내용과 관련된 연습문제 풀기, 읽기, 단어 암기, 쓰기 및 인터넷을 이용하여 관련 정보 찾아 정리하기, 포트폴리오 만들기와 같은 숙제를 내주어 수업시간에 배운 내용을 복습하고 자기 주도적으로 공부 할 수 있도록 한다.

### Dialogue Practice ①

T: Now, I'll give you the homework. Are you ready to write it down?

Ss: Yes.

T: The homework is to practice today's dialogue three times.
Next class, we'll do it in pairs.

S: (raises his/her hand) How many times?

T: I guess you weren't listening.
Everyone, how many times did I say?

Ss: Three times.

T: Right. You need to practice the dialogue three times.

### Dialogue Practice ②

T: Now, look at the screen again. There's today's homework. If you had got more than three points, read the next passage in page 151. And the rest of you have to write down the passage once and read the next passage.

Ss: Okay, we will.

### Pattern Practice

1

| | | |
|---|---|---|
| I'll give you<br>I'll talk about<br>Let me give you<br>Now here's | the homework, | now. |

**2**

| The homework is to<br>For homework,<br>For homework, I want you to<br>Your homework is to | practice today's dialogue five times. |
|---|---|

**3**

| At home,<br>Tonight, | not now, | do<br>learn<br>write<br>practice<br>read<br>revise | the work we've done in class.<br>this dialogue.<br>the exercise on page 9. |
|---|---|---|---|

## Useful Expressions

| 숙제 내주기 | ■ This chapter/lesson/page/exercise is your homework.<br>■ Memorize this dialogue.<br>■ Please practice it over and over.<br>■ This is your homework for today.<br>■ Write the sentences from this page ten times.<br>■ First, fill in the table and then, write the sentences in the blanks.<br>■ Make five sentences using "I want to..."<br>■ Find out the meaning of these words and write them in your notebook.<br>■ Please do this for homework.<br>■ For your homework, make a story based on this dialogue.<br>■ I'll go over it next class.<br>■ Please hand in the homework by Wednesday.<br>= Can you turn it on/by Wednesday?<br>= This assignment is due on/by Wednesday.<br>= I want it handed in on/by Wednesday.<br>■ Do the rest of the exercise as your homework.<br>■ You will have to/must read the last paragraph at home.<br>■ Finish the question you're working on at the moment, and do the rest at home.<br>■ I'm not going to give you any homework today.<br>■ Memorize this dialogue.<br>■ Finish off this exercise at home.<br>■ Don't forget your homework. |
|---|---|

| 숙제 내주기 | ■ Will you read this page five times at home?<br>■ I want you to listen to the CD of today's lesson ten times.<br>■ Please review what we've learned in the class.<br>■ I'm not going to give you any homework this time. |
|---|---|

## 5) 다음 수업 예고하기 (Setting up for Next Class)

수업시간에 배운 내용과 연계하여 다음 시간에 배울 내용을 알려주어 미리 예습하고 관련 자료를 찾아볼 수 있도록 하고, 다음시간에 필요한 준비물 및 수업장소, 시간 등의 변경을 예고한다.

### Dialogue Practice ①

T: Next class, we'll study how to refuse other's suggestions.
Don't forget to bring your book, notebook and file holder.
I'll give you new materials.
Ss: OK.

### Dialogue Practice ②

T: Next class, we will continue to read Min-Su's diaries on pages 85 and 86. Is it clear?
Ss: Yes, it is.

### Pattern Practice

1

| | | |
|---|---|---|
| Will you please remember<br>Don't forget<br>Try not to forget<br>You need<br>Be sure | to bring the money for ____ next lesson<br>to bring scissors and dice to play the game<br>to bring some pictures of your family to class | .(?) |

2

| | | |
|---|---|---|
| Next class, | we'll<br>let's<br>I'll let us | talk about our families. |

## Useful Expressions

| | |
|---|---|
| 다음 수업 예고하기 | ■ We'll do the rest of the lesson next week.<br>■ We'll continue this lesson next time.<br>■ Please bring some pictures of your family to class.<br>■ You will need your/a text book, notebook and some color pencils next class.<br>■ There is a listening quiz next class.<br>■ We are going to learn about the past tense next class.<br>■ Tomorrow we will review.<br>■ There's a change of room for next class.<br>■ Tomorrow we'll meet in the language lab. |

# Part Ⅱ

# 학교 영어

## *School English*

## 1. 국경일 (Holidays and Observances)

전체학생이 모여서 국경일 기념식을 거행하거나, 명절, 기념일 행사를 안내할 때 쓸 수 있는 표현이다,

### 1) 삼일절 (Independence Movement Day)

Presider: 지금부터 삼일절 기념식을 시작하겠습니다. 모두 자리에서 일어나 국기를 향해 주십시오.

》 We will begin the Memorial Service for the Independence Movement Day. All rise. Please turn and face the national flag.

*(When the music is over)*

나라를 위해 목숨을 바친 호국영령을 위해 묵념을 올리겠습니다.

》 In memory of the patriots who devoted and sacrificed themselves for the nation, we will have a moment of silence.

Presider: 교장선생님의 훈화 말씀이 있겠습니다.

》 The principal will deliver the memorial message for the Independence Movement Day.

Principal: 제 89회 삼일절을 맞이하여 오늘 우리는 역사적인 비폭력 독립운동을 기념하기 위해 이 자리에 모였습니다. 이 나라의 독립을 위해 몸

바치신 분들께 진정으로 감사를 드려야 합니다. 선열들이 하셨던 것처럼 나라를 사랑하고 이 나라를 위해 할 수 있는 것을 우리도 하여야 합니다. 이 점을 꼭 명심하고 이러한 삼일정신이 지속될 수 있도록 합시다. 감사합니다.

>>> Today is the 89th anniversary of the Independence Movement Day, so we are gathered together to celebrate this historic non-violent movement. All of us should pay homage to those who sacrificed themselves in restoring the independence of this nation. As our forefathers did, we also should love the nation and do what we can do for our country. Please keep this in mind and let this spirit live on. Please observe this day in earnest. Thank you.

Presider: 이제 모든 기념식이 끝났습니다. 학생들은 담임선생님과 만난 후 귀가하도록 합니다. 해산하시기 바랍니다.

>>> Now the ceremony is over. After meeting with your homeroom teachers, you may go home. You are dismissed.

## 2) 식목일 (Arbor Day)

이번 금요일은 식목일입니다. 집에서 나무를 심거나 식목행사에 참여하십시오. 나무심기 봉사활동을 신청한 학생들은 당일 아침 8시까지 교문 앞에 나오기 바랍니다.

>>> This Friday is Arbor Day. Please plant a seedling at home or join tree planting events. The students who volunteered to plant trees are to be at the school gate by 8 a.m.

나무는 심는 것만큼 정성스레 가꾸는 것도 중요합니다. 교내에 심은 꽃과

나무를 꺾지 말고 잘 가꾸도록 합시다.

≫ It's just as important to treat trees with care as it is to plant them. Please do not pick flowers or break branches off the trees on the school's campus.

화단의 나무나 꽃에 이틀에 한번 씩 물을 주기 바랍니다.

≫ Please water trees and flowers well every other day.

### 3) 어린이날 (Children's Day)

내일은 어린이날입니다. 어린이날은 아동문학가인 방정환 선생님께서 어린이들에게 민족적 자긍심과 독립의식을 불어넣고자 1923년 5월 1일 어린이날을 공포하고 기념행사를 치름으로써 시작되었습니다. 어린이날은 어린이의 인격을 소중히 여기고, 어린이에 대한 사랑과 관심, 존경의 필요성을 강조하는 날입니다. 또한 어린이의 삶을 개선하기 위해 기여한 어른들을 기념하는 날입니다. 미래 사회의 주역인 어린이들을 존중하고 재능을 마음껏 펼칠 수 있도록 어린이들에게 꿈과 희망을 심어줍시다.

≫ Tomorrow is Children's Day. It was founded by the children's writer Bang Jeong-Hwan on May 1, 1923 as a way to instill in children a sense of independence and national pride. Children's Day highlights the dignity of children and their need for love, care, and respect. It is also a day to honor adults that have contributed to improving the lives of children. Children are the future of our nation. Let's show respect for children and inspire them to have dreams and hope so that they can fulfill their potential to the fullest.

올해는 어린이날이 금요일이어서 긴 휴일을 보내게 됩니다. 좋은 계획을 짜서 알차게 보내도록 하기 바랍니다.

Fortunately, Children's Day falls on Friday this year. You will have a long weekend. Prepare a workable plan and make your holidays productive.

중간고사가 임박해 있으므로 집에서 시험 준비를 하면서 보내기 바랍니다.

As you know, the mid-term exams are close at hand, so spend your time preparing for the exams.

## 4) 어버이날 (Parents' Day)

내일은 어버이날입니다. 이날은 무조건적인 사랑으로 우리를 길러 주시고 보다 나은 환경에서 우리를 기르기 위해 자신을 희생하시는 부모님의 사랑을 높이 새기는 날입니다.

Tomorrow is Parents' Day. Parents' Day is a time to celebrate our dedicated parents who strive to raise their children with unconditional love, often putting self-gratification aside to nurture their children in a loving environment.

나를 낳아 길러주신 어버이 은혜에 감사하며, 부모님께 정성이 가득 담긴 감사편지를 쓰도록 합시다.

Thank your parents for what they have done for you since your birth and write a Thank-you letter to them, please.

내일 아침 등교하기 전에 부모님께 카네이션을 달아드리고 감사하다는 말을 하는 것을 잊지 않도록 하십시오. 여러분의 조그마한 몸짓이 부모님께는 큰 행복이 될 수 있습니다.

>>> Tomorrow morning, before you come to school, please pin carnations on your parents and don't forget to say "Thank you." This little gesture will make them very happy.

최근 들어 어버이날의 원래 의미가 퇴색되고 있습니다. 단순히 꽃 한 송이 달아드리는 것으로 끝내지 말고 부모님께 여러분의 사랑을 전하여 이 날을 특별하게 만들어 봅시다.

>>> Nowadays, Parents' Day has lost its original meaning. Instead of a token gesture of flowers, try to make this day special by showing your love for them.

### 5) 스승의 날 (Teacher's Day)

내일은 스승의 날입니다. 스승 찾아뵙기, 모교 방문하기, 안부편지 보내기, 전화하기 등을 통해 스승의 조건 없는 사랑과 배려에 대해 감사하기 바랍니다.

>>> Tomorrow is Teachers' Day. Appreciate your teachers for their unconditional support & efforts by visiting them and your alma mater, calling them or sending letters to them.

스승의 날 기념식이 있겠습니다. 교장선생님께서 교육에 헌신 전념하는 김민수 선생님께 교육과학기술부에서 선정한 우수교원 표창 수여식이 있겠습니다.

>>> We will have a ceremony to celebrate Teachers' Day. Now, the principal will present an award to the most dedicated teacher, Mr. Kim Min-Su designated by the Ministry of Education, Science and Technology.

학생 대표가 선생님의 은혜에 감사하는 편지를 낭독하겠습니다.

>>> The president of the Students' Council will read a letter of appreciation to the teachers.

다음은 다같이 '스승의 은혜' 노래를 부르겠습니다.

>>> Next we will sing the song, 'Grace of the Teachers'.

## 6) 현충일 (Memorial Day)

내일은 현충일입니다. 이 나라를 지키기 위해 목숨을 바치신 선열들을 기리면서, 경건하게 하루를 보내기 바랍니다.

>>> Tomorrow is Memorial Day. Observe this day in a solemn manner, remembering the patriotic ancestors who sacrificed themselves to defend this nation.

현충일에는 조기를 달도록 합시다. 10시에 사이렌이 울리면 하던 일을 멈추고, 조국을 위해 목숨을 바친 선열들을 생각하며 1분간 묵념을 하도록 합니다.

>>> On Memorial Day, we hoist the flag at half-mast. When you hear the

siren at 10 a.m., please stop what you are doing and observe one minute's silent prayer for those who died for this nation.

내일은 국경일입니다. 모두 국기를 게양하고 경건한 마음으로 하루를 보냅시다.

>>> Tomorrow is a national holiday. Please hoist the national flag, and spend the day in a solemn manner.

## 7) 제헌절 (Constitution Day)

내일은 제헌절입니다. 법과 규정을 지키는 것은 민주시민이 되기 위한 가장 중요한 요건이라 할 수 있습니다. 나는 과연 교칙을 잘 지키고 있는지 되돌아보고, 학생다운 면모를 갖추도록 노력합시다.

>>> Tomorrow is Constitution Day. Observation of the laws and the regulations is the No. 1 priority for law-abiding citizens. Please look around yourself and ask if you have observed school regulations well. Be well-behaved students.

제헌절은 광복 3년 후 1948년 최초로 민주주의 선거를 통해 국회를 구성하고 헌법을 제정한 것을 기념하는 날입니다. 2008년부터 더 이상 국경일로 기념하지는 않지만, 헌법의 중요성을 깨닫고 법질서를 존중합시다.

>>> Constitution Day is the day to commemorate the proclamation of the Korean Constitution in 1948, which was three years after the defeat of Japan in World War II and after the first democratic elections and selection of members for the National Assembly. Although Constitution

Day will no longer be a day off for workers beginning in 2008, let us remember the importance of the Constitution and respect the legal order.

## 8) 광복절 (Independence Day)

8월 15일 광복절입니다. 광복절은 우리나라가 일제의 강점으로부터 벗어나 독립국으로서 정부가 수립된 날을 기념하기 위한 날로 1949년부터 매년 8월 15일 기념행사를 치르고 있습니다.

≫ August 15 is Independence Day. It commemorates the freedom from decades of Japanese occupation and the formation of the Republic of Korea in 1949.

조국의 독립을 위해서 살신성인하신 애국지사 및 유공자들께 감사하는 태도를 지녀야겠습니다. 그들의 고귀한 정신을 계승해야 하겠습니다.

≫ We should give thanks to the patriots who devoted themselves to the independence of this nation and the ones who willingly gave up their lives. We should keep their spirit alive.

## 9) 추석 (Chuseok)

오는 25일은 풍년과 조상의 은덕을 기리는 추석입니다. 웃어른을 찾아뵙고 성묘도 합시다. 집에서는 부모님의 일손을 거들어 드리도록 합시다.

≫ September 25 is Chuseok, the Korean Thanksgiving Day, celebrating the good harvest and paying respects to the spirits of our ancestors. Visit the elders in your family and your ancestral graves, too. Please help your mother by doing household chores.

3일간의 추석 연휴를 보람되게 보내기 바랍니다. 그 동안 못했던 과제를 정리하는 기회로 사용하기 바랍니다.

>>> Spend the three-day-long Chuseok break meaningfully. Take advantage of this holiday time to make up for any work you haven't finished.

성묘 갈 때 벌에 쏘이거나 뱀에 물리지 않도록 유의하고, 추석 연휴동안 식중독을 조심하고 과식하지 않도록 합시다.

>>> Please stay safe from bees and snakes when you visit your ancestors' tombs. Please don't overeat and be careful of food poisoning during the Chuseok holiday.

## 10) 개천절 (National Foundation Day)

오는 3일은 개천절입니다. BC 2333년 단군 왕검이 고조선을 설립한 것을 기념하는 날입니다. 반만년의 유구한 역사를 지닌 우리나라에 대한 자부심을 가져야 하겠습니다.

>>> October 3 is National Foundation Day. This holiday celebrates the creation of the state of Gojoseon (Modern-day Korea) founded by Dangun Wanggeom in the year 2333 BC. We should be proud of our nation's 5,000 year-long history.

## 11) 한글날 (Hangul Day)

오는 9일은 한글날입니다. 우리말과 글을 사랑합시다. 최근 들어 한글 경시 풍조가 성행하고 있습니다. 노래 가사, 상표, 간판 이름들이 영어나 국적 불명의 말로 가득 차있습니다. 가장 과학적인 언어로 세계에 알려진 우리말을 사랑하는 태도를 가져야겠습니다.

>>> October 9 is Hangul Day. We should love our language. Nowadays, we tend to think lightly of our language, which is sad. Words in songs, brand names, sign boards are filled with English or other languages whose origins are not known. We should love our language, known as the most scientific language in the world.

영어를 잘 하는 것이 마치 지식인의 표상이라고 생각하는 사람들이 많이 있습니다. 그리고 대화중에 영어 단어를 의도적으로 사용하는 사람들도 많습니다. 우리말을 아끼고 다듬어 쓰면서 이런 바람직하지 못한 습관에서 벗어나도록 노력합시다.

>>> Many people think that speaking English well is a token of being an intellectual. There are also many people who intentionally use English words in their conversation to show off their knowledge. We have to try to avoid this undesirable habit by loving our language and using it correctly.

한글날을 맞이하여 오늘 오후에 시와 수필 부문에 걸쳐 백일장을 열겠습니다. 학생들은 원고지와 필기도구를 준비해서 원하는 장소에서 글을 써 주시기 바랍니다.

>>> To commemorate Hangul Proclamation Day, this afternoon we will hold

a writing contest on the category of poetry and essays. Students are requested to bring writing paper and pens and do your writing wherever you want.

## 12) 학생의 날 (Students' day)

다음 주 월요일은 학생의 날입니다. 1929년 11월 3일 일제 식민주의에 항거해서 일어난 광주 학생 독립운동을 발단으로 전국규모로 확산된 민족 저항 운동을 기념하기 위한 날입니다.

» Next Monday is Students' Day. The "Kwangju Students Independence Movement" that erupted on November 3, 1929 and spread nation-wide, was a national resistance movement against the cruel rule of Japanese colonialism.

학생의 날을 기념하여 모범 학생들을 추천하여 시상하고자 합니다. 적합한 학생이 있으면 생각해보고 추천하기 바랍니다.

» To commemorate this day, we are going to recognize the students who have set good examples for their friends and honor them with prizes. Please think about who would be suitable students and nominate them.

## 13) 설 (Lunar New Year's Day)

오는 2월 8일은 설날입니다. 가족의 소중함과 조상의 은혜를 기리는 동시에, 어려운 이웃도 생각할 수 있는 시간을 갖기 바랍니다.

» The 8th of February is Lunar New Year's Day. Let's think about the importance of family and appreciate what your parents have done for you. Pay respect to your ancestors too. Look around yourself and help those in need.

학년말이 다가오고 있습니다. 해이해지기 쉬운 이때, 올해를 잘 마무리하고 다음 해를 보람차게 맞이하도록 하루하루를 열심히 보내기 바랍니다.

» The end of the school year is drawing near. You are likely to feel like slacking off, but make each day meaningful, finishing the year with good results and preparing for the next year with great expectation.

## 2. 학교 연례행사 (Regular School Events)

입학식, 소풍, 수학여행, 체육대회 및 축제와 같은 학교 연례행사를 안내할 때 쓸 수 있는 표현이다.

### 1) 입학식 (Entrance Ceremony)

10시에 강당에서 입학식을 거행하겠습니다.

» There will be an entrance ceremony in the gym at 10.

신입생들과 학부모님들은 지금 강당으로 들어오셔서 지정된 곳에 자리해 주시기 바랍니다.

It would be appreciated if the freshmen and their parents would come into the gym right away and be seated in the reserved[designated] section.

신입생들은 중간에 서고 2학년은 왼쪽, 3학년은 오른쪽에 서기 바랍니다.

Freshmen, please stand in the middle, Second graders on the left, and third graders on the right, please.

입학식 예행연습을 시작하겠습니다.

We will begin the dress rehearsal for the Entrance Ceremony.

교장 선생님의 환영사가 있겠습니다.

The principal will deliver a welcome address.

여러분들이 우리 학교에 온 것을 진심으로 축하드립니다.

We are happy to have you with us.

신입생 여러분들을 진심으로 축하합니다.

Welcome all of you freshmen from the bottom of my heart.

교감 선생님께서 학교 현황 및 연혁을 소개해 주시겠습니다.

>>> The vice principal will outline the facts and figures of the school and the school's history.

교감선생님께서 신입생 현황을 말씀하시겠습니다.

>>> The vice principal will present the information to the freshmen.

신입생 대표로 김영수군이 선서를 하겠습니다.

>>> The representative of the freshmen, Kim Young-Su will take an oath.

신입생을 대표해서 김영수군이 학칙을 준수하고 책임감 있는 학생으로 행동하겠다는 선서를 하겠습니다. 신입생들은 김영수군이 선서를 하는 동안 오른 손을 들고 있기 바랍니다. 선서가 끝나면 손을 내려 주기 바랍니다.

>>> Kim Young-Su, on behalf of all the freshmen, will pledge them to observe school regulations and conduct themselves as responsible students. While he reads the pledge, all of the freshmen are to raise your right hands. When he finishes, lower your hands.

교감선생님께서 새로 오신 선생님들을 소개해 드리겠습니다. 새로 오신 선생님들은 단상에 올라오셔서 일렬로 서 주시기 바랍니다.

>>> The vice principal will introduce the new teachers to you. New teachers, come up to the podium and line up, please.

올해 우리 학교에 13분의 선생님이 새로 오셨습니다. 그럼 여러분이 보는 곳에서 좌측에서부터 소개를 하겠습니다.

》 This year, we have 13 new teachers. I will introduce them beginning on your left.

새로 오신 선생님들에게 큰 박수를 보내주십시오.

》 Please give all the new teachers a big hand.
Why don't we give the new teachers a big hand?

김은영 선생님께서 새로 오신 선생님들을 대표해서 인사 말씀을 드리겠습니다. 박수로 맞이해 주시기 바랍니다.

》 Kim Eun-Young will deliver her maiden speech to you on behalf of the new teachers. Please give her a big hand.

## 2) 개교기념일 (School Birthday)

3월 5일은 개교기념일인 관계로 임시 휴교입니다. 개교 10주년 기념일을 맞이하여 다시금 학교에 대한 자부심을 갖도록 합시다. 그리고 우리 학교가 멋진 학교가 되고 훌륭한 전통을 세우도록 각자 노력해야겠습니다.

》 March 5 commemorates the opening of the school, so we will have no classes. Celebrating the 10th school birthday, all of us should be proud of our school. We will have to do our best to make this school famous and establish a good tradition.

### 3) 소풍 (School Picnic)

내일 2 · 3학년 소풍이 계획되어 있습니다. 각 학년별 모이는 장소는 2학년 무등산으로, 3학년은 패밀리공원입니다. 9시 30분까지 집합장소로 오기 바라며, 복장은 학생답게 간편하게 오기 바랍니다.

Tomorrow, the second and third grade students will go on a picnic. The second grade students will meet at Mt. Mudeung and the third grade students will get together at the Family Park. You should come to your rendezvous place no later than 9:30 and dress casually. Remember, however, that you are still students and dress appropriately.

학생들은 비닐 봉투를 하나씩 가져오기 바랍니다. 소풍을 마치고 자연 보호 활동을 하겠습니다. 플라스틱 도시락이나 종이컵과 같은 1회 용품은 가능한 한 가져오지 말아 주십시오.

All students are required to bring plastic bags. After the picnic, you will do nature preservation activities. Please don't bring disposable items, such as plastic lunch boxes, paper cups, etc.

소풍 장소에 어떻게 가는지 확실히 알아 놓고 지각하지 않도록 하십시오.

Please make sure you know how to get to your picnic area and be on time.

반별 장기 자랑이 있을 예정이니 각 반은 준비하시기 바랍니다. 공연 시간은 약 10분 정도입니다.

We will have time for each class to dance, sing, present skits and so on, so please be prepared for this. Each class is given 10 minutes, so your presentation should not be longer than that.

내일 일기예보에 따르면 비가 온다고 합니다. 비가 많이 내릴 시 학교에 집합하시기 바랍니다. 비가 조금 내릴 경우에는 예정대로 소풍을 가도록 하겠습니다.

≫ The weather forecast said it will rain tomorrow. In case of heavy rain, please come to school, otherwise, go to your picnic as planned.

우천 시를 대비해서 비상 연락망을 확인하기 바랍니다. 누구에게서 연락을 받고 누구에게 연락할 것인지를 확인하세요. 비가 내릴 경우에 학교나 담임선생님께 전화를 해 보기 바랍니다.

≫ In case of rain, please check the emergency communication network. Please make sure who is before and after you in the network. If you are not sure, call your homeroom teacher at school.

만일의 사태를 대비해서 반별로 응급처치 구호품을 준비하시기 바랍니다.

≫ In case of accidents, each class should bring a first-aid kit.

## 4) 수학여행 (Field Trip)

1학년 학생들을 대상으로 알려드립니다. 오늘 3교시 후 강당에서 수학여행과 관련하여, 교감선생님의 훈화 말씀이 있으니 3교시 마치는 대로 강당으로 이동해 주기 바랍니다.

≫ An announcement will be made to the first grade students. Please go to the auditorium directly after the third period. The vice principal will give you instructions regarding the upcoming field trip, so please gather together in the gym immediately after the third class.

매년 이맘때 쯤이면 날씨가 변덕스럽습니다. 춥거나 비가 올 경우를 대비해 두꺼운 옷과 우산을 준비해 오기 바랍니다. 감기약, 멀미약 같은 개인 상비약도 함께 준비해 오기 바랍니다.

The weather at this time of year is very unpredictable. Don't forget to bring umbrellas and warm clothes. Also bring medicine for colds or travel sickness.

유의 사항을 한번 더 알려드리겠습니다. 내일 출발 시간을 엄수해 주시고 숙소 전화번호와 도착 시간을 부모님께 알려 드리기 바랍니다.

Allow me to repeat the things you have to remember. Please come to the rendezvous place on time. Also, please let your parents know the telephone numbers of the hotels and the arrival time.

필요 이상의 돈을 소지하지 않도록 하기 바랍니다. 금전 분실 사고에 대비해서 용돈은 담임선생님께 맡겨 놓으시고 절대로 방에 그냥 두지 않도록 하십시오.

Please don't carry more money than you need. To prevent loss of money, please deposit it with your teacher. Never leave money unattended in your room.

산을 오를 때는 서두르거나 뛰지 마십시오. 돌에 걸려 넘어지거나 미끄러운 돌을 밟아 낙상을 입을 수 있습니다. 차를 탈 때도 차례로 타고 내리도록 합시다. 안전사고 없이 수학여행을 마칠 수 있도록 여러분이 협조해 주기 바랍니다.

>>> When you hike in the mountains, walk slowly and never run. Be careful not to stumble or fall on slippery stones. Get on and off the buses in single file. Your cooperation is essential to making this field trip successful without anyone getting hurt.

2·3학년 학생들에게 알립니다. 내일부터 2박 3일간 1학년 학생들이 제주도로 수학여행을 떠납니다. 이들이 없는 동안 1학년 교실 쪽으로의 출입을 자제해 주기 바랍니다.

>>> This is an announcement for the second and third grade students. The first grade students will be going on a field trip to Jeju Island for two nights and three days. No one is allowed near the first grade classrooms during their absence.

## 5) 학생 간부 수련회 (Leadership Program)

수련회에 참가할 학생회 간부들은 식사 후 1시 20분에 회의실로 모여주기 바랍니다.

>>> The student representatives who will participate in the training program are asked to get together in the conference room at 1:20 p.m. after lunch.

수련회에 참가할 학생회 간부들은 수련원 생활에 필요한 물품들을 챙겨서 내일 아침 9시까지 수련원에 도착하기 바랍니다. 질문이 있으면 교무실 학생지도부 부장선생님께 물어보시기 바랍니다.

>>> The student representatives taking part in the training program are expected to bring all the necessary items they will need during the program. We will meet at the training center at 9 a.m. tomorrow morning. If you have any questions, please ask the Dean of Students' Affairs and Guidance.

## 6) 체육대회 (Track and Field Day)

개교기념일을 기념하여 체육대회를 하겠습니다. 세부사항에 대해선 체육선생님께서 프로그램을 나누어 주시겠습니다. 각 반별로 체육대회 참가 계획을 잘 세워서 의미 있는 체육대회가 되도록 해주시기 바랍니다.

>>> In celebration of the school foundation day, an athletic meeting will take place. The physical education teacher will hand out the specifics of the meeting. Each class should make a thorough plan for it and help make the meeting meaningful.

이번주 금요일부터 체육대회 예선 경기가 시작됩니다. 경기 종목은 줄다리기, 800미터 릴레이, 축구, 단체 줄넘기, 이인삼각 등으로 다양합니다. 출전선수 명단을 늦어도 목요일까지 체육선생님께 제출하기 바랍니다.

>>> The preliminary games will start this Friday. The events you will participate in will be a tug-of-war, 800-meter relay race, soccer, group rope jumping, three-legged race, and so on. Please hand in the lists of participants to the physical education teacher no later than Thursday.

각 반 학생들은 원활한 대회 진행을 위해서 방송이 나가면 응원을 잠시 멈추고 다음에 어떤 경기가 열리는지 귀 기울여 주시기 바랍니다. 그리고 해당 게임이 열리면 즉각 해당 장소로 모이기 바랍니다.

>>> To make the meeting go smoothly, when an announcement is made over the intercom, stop cheering and listen. When the events you are involved in are to begin, please hurry to the selected locations.

잠시 후 800미터 릴레이 경기가 진행됩니다. 선수들은 운동장 출발선 앞으로 나오기 바랍니다.

>>> The 800-meter relay will take place soon. The runners are asked to come to the start line in the grounds.

곧 줄다리기 준결승전이 벌어집니다. 준결승에 참가하는 학급들은 운동장 가운데로 나와서 준비하기 바랍니다.

>>> The semifinal of the tug-of-war will be held in a minute. The classes involved are to come to the middle of the field and get ready for the event.

이로써 오전 경기가 모두 끝이 났습니다. 학생들은 점심을 먹고 2시까지 운동장에 다시 모이기 바랍니다.

>>> All the morning events are over. Have lunch and come back to your areas at 2.

축구 결승전이 3시에 진행됩니다. 선수들은 준비를 해 있다가 안내 방송이 나가면 즉시 운동장에 모이기 바랍니다.

»» The final game of soccer will be held at 3 p.m. The players are asked to get ready and come to the field right away at the announcement.

학생들과 선생님들 간에 소프트볼 경기가 있겠습니다. 선수들은 입장하시기 바랍니다.

»» There will be a softball game between the teachers and the students. The players are requested to come forward now.

이번 체육대회 최우수 학반은 3학년 2반입니다. 실장은 앞으로 나오기 바랍니다.

»» The first prize in this athletic meeting goes to Class 3-2. Will the class president, please come forward?

응원상은 2학년 4반이 받겠습니다.

»» The prize for cheering goes to Class 2-4.

체육대회가 끝이 났습니다. 의자는 모두 교실에 갖다 두고 다시 나와서 운동장 청소를 하기 바랍니다. 운동장을 원래 상태대로 깨끗이 청소하기 바랍니다.

»» The athletic meet is over. Please put your chairs back in your classrooms and go back to the field and pick up the trash. Leave the field as clean as it was before we started.

## 7) 여름방학 (Summer Vacation)

7월 19일부터 8월 24일까지 하계 방학이 실시됩니다. 이 기간 동안 자신의 건강을 다지는 동시에 미흡했던 과목을 보충하여 2학기를 대비하도록 합시다. 그리고 물놀이를 할 때 안전수칙을 잘 지켜 불의의 사고를 예방하도록 합시다.

≫ Summer vacation will start on July 19, finishing on August 24. During this period, stay in shape by maintaining a balanced diet. Prepare for the fall semester, and review your weaker subjects. When you go swimming, be fully aware of safety guidelines to prevent accidents.

방학동안 봉사 활동에 참여할 계획을 세우기 바랍니다. 봉사활동을 할 수 있는 기관에 대한 정보는 담임선생님께 물어 보십시오.

≫ Make a plan to take part in a volunteer program. If you need any information about volunteer work, please ask your homeroom teacher.

방학 중 방과 후 교육은 7월 28일부터 3주간 실시될 것입니다. 아침 9시에 시작이 되며 하루에 5시간 수업을 하게 됩니다. 부모님 동의서를 다음 주 월요일까지 가져오기 바랍니다.

≫ After-school classes during the vacation will be carried out for three weeks, starting on July 28. The classes will start at 9 and there will be 5 classes each day. Please don't forget to bring back parental permission forms for the classes next Monday.

방학 중 등교 시 교복을 꼭 입도록 합니다. 머리를 염색하거나 귀를 뚫고 귀걸이를 하는 일이 없도록 합시다.

>>> When you come to school during the vacation, please wear your school uniform. Please don't dye your hair or pierce your ears and wear earrings.

각종 단체에서 행하는 행사에 참가하는 학생들은 확인서를 담임선생님께 제출하기 바랍니다. 부모님 허락 없이 캠핑을 가는 일이 없도록 합시다.

>>> All of the students who are planning to join various camps are to hand in a confirmation of participation note to your homeroom teachers. Don't go hiking or camping without parental permission.

술을 마시거나 부탄가스 흡입 등을 하지 않도록 합시다. 이는 여러분의 건강에 해롭습니다. 가스 흡입을 하다가 폭발 사고로 큰 피해를 입을 수 있으니 절대로 이런 행동을 하지 않도록 하기 바랍니다.

>>> Don't drink alcohol or experiment with butane gas or solvents. This is really bad for your health. In particular, gas can explode, causing you severe damage to you. Don't even think about it.

본드나 부탄가스 흡입은 여러분을 일시적으로 기분 좋게 할지 모르나 뇌에는 영구적으로 치명적인 상해를 가하게 되니 절대 이런 일이 없도록 합시다. 순간의 쾌락이 영원한 상처를 남길 수 있다는 사실을 명심하기 바랍니다.

>>> Sniffing glue or butane gas can cause temporary hallucinations, but it can also permanently damage your brain. Never do this stupid thing. Please remember pursuing temporary pleasure can lead to permanent misery.

지나친 컴퓨터 사용은 여러분의 건강을 해칩니다. 폭력적이고 선정적인 컴퓨터 게임과 유해사이트 방문을 하지 맙시다. 인터넷 중독에 빠지지 않도록 컴퓨터 사용시간을 정해서 이용하도록 합시다.

》 Too much computer use harms your health. Do not play violent computer games or visit obscene Web sites. Please set a limited time to use the computer in order not to become addicted to the Internet.

## 8) 개학식 (First Day of the New Semester)

오늘부터 2학기가 시작됩니다. 새로운 마음으로 알찬 2학기가 되도록 최선을 다 합시다.

》 The fall semester begins today. Let's make this semester a productive one with renewed energy.

오늘 1교시는 강당에서 시업식을 하고 2교시는 교실 청소를 하고 3교시부터 정상 수업을 하겠습니다.

》 We will have the opening ceremony in the first period, and clean up the classrooms in the second period. From the third period, you will have regular classes as usual.

오늘 계획된 특기 적성 교육은 토요일 아침 8시에 실시하겠습니다. 착오 없으시기 바랍니다.

》 The class for special skills and aptitude planned for today will instead take place at 8 a. m. this Saturday. Please don't get confused.
Today's class for special skills and aptitude will be shifted to 8 a.m. this Saturday. Please don't forget this.

## 9) 축제 (School Festival)

오는 14일부터 16일까지 학교축제가 예정되어 있습니다. 우리 학교를 대외에 알릴 수 있는 좋은 기회입니다. 손님들이 좋은 기억을 갖고 돌아갈 수 있도록 최선을 다합시다.

The school festival is scheduled to be held from the 14th to 16th. It will give us a good chance to advertise our school to others. Let's do our best to make a good impression on the visitors.

제일고등학교 방송실입니다. 지금부터 방송제를 시작하겠습니다. 모두 즐거운 시간이 되길 바랍니다.

This is the Je-il High School broadcasting station. Now we are beginning our broadcasting festival. I hope you will have a good time..

불우이웃 돕기 바자회가 강당에서 열립니다. 판매 수익금 모두는 불우이웃들을 위해서 쓰일 것입니다. 적극적으로 참여해 주면 고맙겠습니다.

The bazaar for the less fortunate will be held in the gym. The profits from it will be used for people in need. Your generous participation would be appreciated.

축제 기간 중에 알뜰 시장이 열릴 것입니다. 집에서 사용하지 않는 물건들을 가져오시기 바랍니다. 여러분에게 필요하지 않은 물건들이 다른 사람들에게는 유용할 수도 있습니다. 그리고 모든 수익금은 불우이웃 돕기에 쓰일 것입니다.

During the school festival, there will be a flea market. Please bring things you don't need at your home. These items may be useful to other people. This is a charity event, so all the profit goes to helping the less fortunate.

다양한 프로그램이 준비되어 있습니다. 차분히 구경하시고 다양한 행사들을 즐기시길 바랍니다. 혹시 책자가 필요하시면 안내센터로 오시기 바랍니다.

≫ We have various programs. Take your time and enjoy all the events. If you need a brochure, please come to the information desk.

축제 마감 시간이 다가오고 있습니다. 관람객들은 서둘러 구경하시고 참가서클들은 마무리할 준비를 하기 바랍니다.

≫ The closing time for the festival is soon. We are sorry, but would the visitors please hurry through and the clubs get ready for closing.

축제 기간 동안 보여준 여러분들의 성원에 감사를 드립니다. 내년엔 더 나은 축제가 되도록 노력하겠습니다. 안녕히 돌아가십시오.

≫ Thank you for the support you have given during the festival. We will make an effort to make next year's festival even better. Please have a safe trip back home.

## 10) 겨울 방학 (Winter Vacation)

12월 29부터 2월 8일까지 동계방학이 실시됩니다. 이번 방학은 다음 학년을 준비하는 기간으로 충실한 계획을 짜서 알차게 보내기 바랍니다.

⋙ Winter vacation will start on Dec. 29, ending on February 8. This vacation is a preparatory period for the next school year. So make a thorough and practical plan and make this vacation productive.

불우 이웃 성금을 모금하겠습니다. 각반별로 성의껏 모아서 금요일까지 담임선생님께 내어 주기 바랍니다.

⋙ There will be a charity drive. Please give the less fortunate as much as you can. When you finish collecting the donations, please take them to your homeroom teachers, no later than Friday.

## 11) 졸업식 (Graduation Ceremony)

오는 2월 12일 졸업식을 거행합니다. 2학년 학생들은 10시까지 강당으로 모여주기 바랍니다. 1학년들은 그날 하루 수업이 없습니다.

⋙ On Feb. 12, we will hold commencements. The second grade students are expected to come to the hall by 10 o'clock. The first grade students have the day off.

각종 시상이 있겠습니다. 상을 받을 학생들은 앞자리에 앉아주기 바랍니다.

⋙ There will be award giving section during the commencements. The students who will receive awards are asked to sit in the front rows.

재학생의 송별사가 있겠습니다.

⋙ A student representative will read the farewell speech to the graduates.

졸업생의 답사가 있겠습니다.

A graduate representative will reply to the speech.

3년간의 학교생활을 마치고 이제 이 학교를 떠나게 됩니다. 우리 학교 졸업생이란 사실에 대해 자부심을 가지고 또한 이곳에서 배운 것들을 잊어버리지 않기 바랍니다.

You are leaving this school after having studied for three years. You should be proud of having been students of this school and keep in mind what you have learned here.

졸업생들은 졸업식은 끝이 아니라 새로운 시작임을 명심하기 바랍니다. 새로운 출발을 하고자 하는 여러분들에게 행운이 함께 하길 바랍니다.

The graduates are asked to bear in mind that the commencement is not an ending but a new beginning. As you start your new life, I wish you good luck.

교감 선생님께서 이번 졸업생의 대학입학 결과를 말씀드리겠습니다.

The vice principal will give the results of how many of the graduates have entered colleges.

## 3. 시험 · 경시대회 (Tests and Contests)

중간고사와 기말고사 및 각종 시험과 경시대회를 안내하고 시상할 때 쓸 수 있는 표현이다.

### 1) 중간고사 (Mid-Term Exams)

오는 5월 4일부터 8일까지 중간고사가 실시됩니다. 최선을 다하되 부정행위는 절대로 없도록 합시다. 시간표는 게시판에 붙어 있습니다.

≫ The mid-term exams are scheduled to begin on May 4th and will go through the 8th. Do your best and never cheat on the exams. The schedule for the exams is posted on the bulletin board.

부정행위 금지

≫ No cheating will be allowed. All cheating will be punished.

책상 위에 아무 것도 쓰지 마세요.

≫ Don't write anything on your desks.

문제지를 다음 학생에게 전해 주세요.

≫ Please pass the exam papers on to the next student.
Please pass the papers back.

컴퓨터용 사인펜을 꼭 준비하기 바랍니다.

Please bring a black marker pen for the computer answer cards.

답안지에 답을 표시할 때 실수를 막기 위해서 푸른 색이나 붉은 색으로 먼저 표시하고 나중에 컴퓨터용 사인펜으로 표기하기 바랍니다.

You can mark your answers with a blue or red pen to prevent errors and remark them with a black marker pen for the computer

푸른 색과 붉은 색은 컴퓨터가 인식을 하지 못하지만 다른 색은 인식을 하므로 사용하지 않기 바랍니다.

Computers can't read red and blue markings, but they can read other colors. Therefore, don't use any colors other than red and blue.

답안지를 제출하기 전에 답안지에 답 표기를 옳게 했는지 확인하세요.

Please make sure that you have marked the answers correctly before turning in your answer card.

절대로 수정액을 사용해서는 안 됩니다.

Never use whiteout on your answer card.

오늘부터 중간고사가 시작됩니다. 각 교실마다 책상 배열을 5줄로 하기 바라며, 각 반의 절반이 다른 학년 교실로 이동합니다.

The mid-term exams start today. Please arrange the desks in 5 columns. Half of the students from each class are to move into another classroom in a different grade.

2교시에 1학년은 자습을 하고 2학년은 시험을 치겠습니다. 1학년 학생들은 2학년의 시험에 방해가 되지 않도록 주의하기 바랍니다.

During the second period, the first grade students will have a self-study hour, while the second grade students will take an exam. The first graders are asked not to disturb the second grade students.

오늘은 시험 마지막 날입니다. 시험은 3교시에 마치겠습니다. 4교시에 교실 청소를 하겠습니다. 시험 기간 동안 하지 못해 더러워진 교실을 깨끗이 청소해 주기 바랍니다.

Today is the last day for the mid-terms. They will finish in the third period, so during the fourth period, please clean up your classrooms which have gotten dirty during the exam period.

그 동안 시험 보느라 수고했습니다. 시험을 마치고 바로 집에 가서 충분한 휴식을 취하기 바랍니다. 내일부터 정상수업을 하겠습니다.

You have done great work on your exams. Please go straight home after the exams and rest. Tomorrow, our schedule will go back to normal.

## 2) 기말고사 (Final Examinations)

7월 7일부터 7월 10일까지 학기말고사가 실시됩니다.

The final exams will be given from July 7 to July 10.

한 학기를 마무리할 시간이 다가오고 있습니다. 한 학기를 보람되게 마칠 수 있도록 남은 기간을 잘 마무리하기 바랍니다.

The closing of this semester is around the corner, so make every effort to finish this semester with satisfactory results by making good use of the remaining days.

한 학기를 마무리 할 시간이 다가옵니다. 쓸데없이 시간을 허비하지 말고 미리 여름방학 계획을 짜도록 합시다.

The end of spring semester is drawing near. Use your time effectively by making your plans for vacation in advance.

시험 결과가 나오면 혹시라도 점수가 잘못 되었는지 확인하기 바랍니다. 점수가 잘못된 경우엔 담당과목 선생님께 가서 답안지 마킹이 제대로 되었는지 확인하기 바랍니다.

When the results of the final exams come out, please check if there are any errors in your marks. If you find errors in a certain subject, go to the teachers in charge of that subject and see if your marks are correct.

### 3) 영어 듣기시험 (English Listening Test)

영어 듣기 시험을 11시에 실시합니다. 시간 조정이 있겠습니다. 변경된 시간표는 게시판에 있으니 참조하시기 바랍니다. 감독관 선생님들은 10분 일찍 들어가셔서 학생들이 시험에 대비하도록 하여 주십시오.

The English listening test will take place at 11 o'clock, so there will be some changes in the schedule. The changed schedule is on the bulletin board. The supervising teachers are asked to go to the classes 10 minutes prior to the bell and get the students ready for the test.

각 반의 감독 선생님들은 방송이 잘 들리는지 확인해 주시기 바랍니다. 이상이 있으면 실장을 방송실로 보내 주십시오.

>>> The supervising teachers are asked to make sure the intercom sounds okay. If there are any problems, please send the class president to the broadcasting room.

번호 순서대로 창문 쪽에서부터 앉기 바랍니다.

>>> Please be seated in numeric order from the window side.

창 쪽에 햇빛이 너무 들어오는데 커튼을 쳐주세요.

>>> There is too much sun on the window side, so please draw the curtains.

11시부터 영어듣기 시험이 실시됩니다. 선생님의 지시사항을 잘 듣고 요구된 사항을 그대로 행하십시오.

>>> The English listening test is starting at 11 o'clock. Please listen carefully to the teacher's directions and do exactly what he or she asks you to do.

오늘은 영어 듣기 시험으로 인해 시간 변경이 있겠습니다. 오전 수업은 10분 일찍 시작하고 3교시는 60분 수업으로 하겠습니다. 그리고 오후 수업은 예전과 같이 하겠습니다.

>>> Today there will be some changes in the timetable because of the English

listening test. Morning classes will start 10 minutes earlier than normal, and the third period will be an hour long. Afternoon classes will be as usual.

수업 중에 죄송합니다. 영어 듣기 방송의 2번 문항이 방송 상태가 나빠서 제대로 들을 수 없었던 관계로 다시 한 번 들려드리겠습니다.

≫ I am sorry for disturbing your class. The second question in the English listening test was difficult to hear because of bad reception, so you will be able to listen to it again from the tape.

영어 듣기 시험이 끝이 났습니다. 답지를 앞으로 내 주시기 바랍니다. 그리고 바로 수업을 시작하시면 되겠습니다. 감사합니다.

≫ The English listening test is over. Please pass the answer sheets forward, then get ready for your regular classes. Thank you for your cooperation.

### 4) 수학능력 평가 (Korean Scholastic Aptitude Test)

오는 11월 12일에는 수학능력평가가 실시되므로 수업이 없습니다. 우리학교가 수학능력시험장으로 활용될 예정이오니 교실에 붙어있는 각종 게시물을 모두 제거하기 바랍니다. 벽에 아무 것도 없게 해 주시기 바랍니다.

≫ There will be no class on November 12th because of the Korean Scholastic Aptitude Test. Some applicants for the Korean Scholastic Aptitude Test will take the exams here in our school on that day. Please remove all posters and papers from the bulletin board. Nothing is to be on the walls, either.

우리학교의 3학년 학생들은 미래고등학교에서 수능시험을 치를 예정입니다. 그 날에 나올 수 있는 학생들은 아침 6시까지 미래고등학교 정문 앞으로 모여 선배들을 응원하도록 합시다.

The Senior students of our school will take the exams in Mirae high school. If you are available on that day, come to the front gate of Mirae high school before 6 a.m. and cheer for your seniors.

## 5) 경시대회 (Academic Contests and Competitions)

(Kind of contests : English, Math, Science, Social studies, and so on.)

오는 5월 9일 교내 (학력)경시대회를 개최하고자 합니다. 각 과목별로 대회에 참가하기를 원하는 학생은 담당 선생님께 신청해 주기 바랍니다.

We will hold school-wide contests in various subjects on May 9th. Students who are interested in the contests are asked to decide which contest they will take part in and then register their name with the teachers involved.

오늘 2시에 영어 경시대회를 개최합니다. 시험 장소는 게시판에 붙어 있습니다. 참가 신청을 한 학생은 10분전까지 시험장소로 모여주기 바랍니다.

The English contest will start at 2 p.m. today. The contest locations are posted on the bulletin board. The applicants should come to the appointed places 10 minutes before the contest begins.

## 6) 환경미화 심사 (Classroom Display Contest)

이번 주 토요일에 환경미화 심사가 있습니다. 교실을 공부할 수 있는 분위기가 넘치는 곳으로 잘 꾸며주시고, 특별구역도 깨끗이 청소해 주십시오.

This Saturday, we will hold a competition to judge the best decorated classroom. Please remember to keep your classroom clean so it can be a pleasant place to study. Also, don't forget you are responsible for your classes' designated cleaning zones.

환경미화 심사 결과를 알려드리겠습니다. 최우수반은 2-1반입니다. 학년별 우수반은 아래와 같습니다.

Class 2-1 is judged the winner of the best decorated classroom competition. The best classrooms of each grade are as follows.

## 7) 시상 (Awards)

다음은 성적이 우수한 학생에게 시상하겠습니다.

Next, the awards will be given to the outstanding students in school-work.

교내 독서토론대회에서 입상한 학생들에 대해 시상하겠습니다.

The awards will be given to those who excelled in a book review debate.

호명하는 학생은 단상으로 올라가기 바랍니다.

Please stand up when your name is called and come up to the stage.

이어서 교내 독후감 발표대회에서 입상한 학생들에게 시상하겠습니다.

>>> Secondly, the prizes for the students with best book review presentation.

다음은 대외상을 전달하겠습니다.

>>> Next, the out-of-school competition prizes are conferred.

먼저 전국 홈페이지 경연대회에서 입상한 학생입니다.

>>> First, these are the students who won prizes in the nation-wide home-page building contest.

다음은 제 4회 한국 생물 올림피아드에서 입상한 학생들입니다.

>>> Next are students who won prizes in the 4th Korean biology Olympiad.

다음은 국제통역사 협회가 주최한 제 9회 외국어 경연대회에서 장려상을 받은 학생들입니다.

>>> Next are students who won prizes in the 9th International Interpreter's competition & Foreign Language contest hosted by the International Interpreter's Association.

다음은 한국대학교와 Korea Post가 공동 주최한 제 1회 전국 영어 에세이 쓰기 경시대회에서 입상한 학생들입니다.

>>> Next are students who won prizes in the first national English essay contest sponsored by Hankook University and the Korea Post.

최우수상: the Most excellent prize
장려상: the Encouragement prize
은상: the silver prize
특별상: the special prize

우수상: the Excellent prize
금상: the gold prize
동상: the bronze prize

**[운동경기]**
우승: the Champion
준우승: the First Runner-up
3위: the Second Runner-up

## 8) 지능 · 적성 검사 (Aptitude Test)

오늘 2~3교시에 걸쳐 1학년 학생을 대상으로 적성 검사를 실시합니다.

>>> The first grade students will take an aptitude test during the second and third period today.
The aptitude test will take place for the first grade students during the Second and third periods.

적성검사로 인해서 시간 변경이 있겠습니다. 선생님들은 바뀐 시간을 확인하시길 바랍니다. 실장은 칠판에 변경된 시간표를 적어 놓기 바랍니다.

>>> There will be some schedule changes due to the aptitude test. The teachers are asked to check the new schedule. Class presidents are to write the changes on the blackboard.

시험은 방송을 통해 치르게 됩니다. 감독하시는 선생님과 학생들은 방송에 귀 기울여 지시사항을 따라 주시기 바랍니다.

>>> The test will be carried out over the intercom. Both the teachers and the students are expected to listen to the intercom with care and follow the directions.

## 4. 교과 외 활동 (Extra-curricula Activities)

방과 후 학교, 계발활동, 아침독서 및 명상, 봉사활동 등의 교과외 활동을 안내할 때 쓸 수 있는 표현이다.

### 1) 방과 후 학교 (After-School Program)

방과 후 교육을 위한 안내 방송이 있겠습니다. 학생들은 각자 관심 있는 분야나 좋아하는 과목을 정하고 등록하기 바랍니다. 한 사람이 최소한 3과목 이상 선택하시기 바랍니다.

≫ The orientation for after-school classes will be broadcasted over the intercom. All students are requested to choose their fields of interest or subjects and register. Each student should choose no less than 3 subjects.

방과 후 교육활동에 참여하지 않는 학생들은 빨리 귀가하고 쓸데없이 돌아다니는 일이 없도록 하기 바랍니다.

≫ The students who don't participate in after-school classes are asked to go straight home. There will be no aimless roaming from place to place.

## 2) 계발활동 (Club Activities)

신학년도 특별활동 부서를 조직하고자 합니다. 자신의 적성과 특기를 살릴 수 있도록 신중하게 생각해 주시기 바랍니다.

≫ We are going to organize the clubs. Please think carefully about which one will help you develop your aptitude and skills.

학생들은 해당 클럽에 가서 등록하기 바랍니다.

≫ Please go to your club and register.

매주 금요일 7교시에 특별활동을 실시합니다.

≫ Club activities will be held during the 7th period every Friday.

오늘은 우천 관계로 특별활동을 실시하지 않습니다.

≫ As it is raining, there will be no club activities.

비가 오는 관계로 야외 활동을 하는 클럽들은 지정된 교실에서 클럽활동을 실시해 주시기 바랍니다.

≫ As it is raining, the clubs which normally meet outdoors are asked to meet in their designated classrooms, instead.

이번달 전일제 클럽활동은 3번째 토요일에 있겠습니다.

≫ The club activities which last the whole day will be held on the third Saturday this month.

이번주 클럽 활동은 다가 오는 시험 때문에 연기됩니다. 대신에 시험이 끝난 후에 2시간을 하겠습니다.

>>> Club activities will be postponed because of the coming exams. Instead, after the exams, we will have club activities for two hours.

교내 축제에 참가하고자 하는 클럽은 미리 참가 계획을 수립해 주시기 바랍니다.

>>> The clubs planning to take part in the school festival are asked to prepare and submit a plan in advance.

## 3) 아침 독서 (Morning Reading)

매일 8시부터 9시까지는 독서 시간입니다. 이 시간에 몇 권을 읽을 것인가 목표를 정해서 노력하십시오. 그리고 다 읽은 책에 대해서는 독후감을 쓰기 바랍니다. 연말에 잘 된 독후감에 대해 시상을 할 예정입니다.

>>> Every day from 8 to 9, you will read books. Please set a goal for the number of books you will read during the time and work toward that goal. Please write a book review on each book you complete. At the end of this year, we will give awards for good book reviews.

아침은 독서하기 좋은 시간입니다. 한 주에 한 권 이상 독서하기를 실천하고 독후감을 쓰도록 합시다.

>>> Morning is a good time for reading. Let's try to read more than one book a week and write book reviews.

한권의 책이 여러분의 미래를 열어줍니다. 독서는 여러분의 공부와 세상에 대한 견문을 넓히는데 도움이 되니 매일 독서를 실천합시다. 아침독서시간을 알차게 보낼 수 있도록 최선의 노력을 다하기 바랍니다.

One book may open your future and reading increases your academic and world knowledge as well. Don't forget each day counts, so make each day productive, please.

### 4) 아침 명상 (Morning Meditation)

매일 아침 8시 40분부터 55분까지는 명상의 시간입니다. 학생들은 하던 일을 멈추고 자리에 앉아 조용히 눈을 감고 방송에 귀를 기울여 주시기 바랍니다. 명상 방송이 끝난 후에는 명상노트에 느낀 점을 기록하도록 합시다.

Every morning from 8:40 through 8:55, we have morning meditation time. Please stop what you are doing now and remain seated with your eyes closed. Please pay attention to the broadcasting and write down what you have felt in your journal after you listen.

### 5) 봉사 활동 (Volunteer Activities)

봉사활동은 어느 누구의 직접적이거나 암시적인 압력 또는 강압 없이 공공단체, 자선, 인권단체를 위해 무료로 봉사하는 활동입니다. 봉사활동에 관한 시간과 장소 문의는 학교 홈페이지 봉사활동란을 참조해주시기 바랍니다.

⋙ Volunteer services must be both offered freely and without pressure or coercion, direct or implied, from anyone, and performed for civic, charitable or humanitarian reasons. If you have any questions about the appropriateness of volunteering time and place, please refer to 'volunteer work' at the school homepage.

봉사활동은 1년에 20시간 이상 사회 봉사기관, 관공서, 자선단체에서 실시하여야합니다. 봉사활동시간은 1일 4시간 이하로 규정합니다. 사설유치원이나 은행과 같은 이익 기관에서의 활동은 봉사활동으로 간주되지 않으니 유의하기 바랍니다.

⋙ Volunteer work time should be more than 20 hours a year and it is restricted to 4 hours a day at maximum. Please keep in mind that any volunteer work at private sectors such as a private kindergarten or a bank is not considered as legal volunteer work.

봉사활동 신청을 받습니다. 봉사활동을 희망하는 학생은 김미영 선생님에게 반, 번호, 성명을 써서 명단을 제출해주기 바랍니다.

⋙ We will recruit students who want to join volunteer activities. If you want to, please go to Miss. Kim Mi-Young and fill out your personal information on the application form.

## 5. 교칙 (School Regulations)

학생으로서 준수해야할 행동 규범과 건강하고 쾌적한 생활을 하기 위해서 유의해야할 사항들을 안내할 때 쓸 수 있는 표현이다.

### 1) 행동 규범 (Code of Conduct)

우리 학교의 모든 학생들은 학기 초에 공지된 교칙을 엄수하길 바랍니다. 몇 가지 중요한 교칙은 다음과 같습니다.

≫ All students are expected to follow the rules and regulations of the school that were given to you at the beginning of the year. Here are some of the most important points from the Discipline Code:

욕설 같은 부적절한 언어의 사용은 금지됩니다.

≫ Using inappropriate language such as vulgar words is not permitted.

교내외 폭력사건의 연루학생은 등교 정지 처리됩니다.

≫ Fighting in school or within the vicinity of school will result in a suspension.

교내의 도난사건 및 기물파손 연루 학생은 해당 금액을 손해배상 해야 하며 등교 정지 처리됩니다.

>>> Any student involved in stealing, vandalizing, or defacing property on school grounds will assume the cost of financial restitution and will face suspension.

- 교내 흡연은 금지되며, 라이터와 성냥은 학교에 가져올 수 없습니다.

>>> Smoking is prohibited on school grounds. Lighters and matches may not be brought to school.

- 휴대전화, mp3 플레이어 및 기타 전자기기는 학습에 방해가 되므로 교내로 가져올 수 없습니다.

>>> Cell phones, mp3 players, and other electronic devices are disruptive to the educational process, and these prohibited items may NOT be brought into the school building.

## 2) 학급 규칙 (Class Rules)

- 모든 학생들은 면학분위기 조성을 위하여 아래의 사항들을 반드시 준수하여 주시기 바랍니다.

>>> Every student must keep the rules below in order to foster learning atmosphere.

- 등교시간을 지킵시다.

>>> Arrive on time.

말하기 전에 손을 듭니다.

Raise your hand before speaking.

다른 학생의 말을 경청하고 학급 토론에 참여 합시다.

Listen to others and participate in class discussions.

과업에 집중하고 과제를 해옵시다.

Stay on task and do your assignments.

수업준비물을 지참하고 미리 수업 준비를 합시다.

Bring materials and have them ready.

교사의 지시사항을 잘 들읍시다.

Listen to directions.

모둠 활동 시 협동합시다.

Cooperate with your group.

다른 학생들의 학습지에 손대지 않습니다.

Leave other people's materials alone.

다른 학생들의 공부를 방해하지 않습니다.

Do not interrupt other students' learning.

- 학교기물을 파손하지 맙시다. 책상이나 학교 재물 위에 낙서를 하지 맙시다.

  ⋙ No vandalism. Don't write on your desk or school property.

- 컴퓨터는 학습용으로만 사용합니다.

  ⋙ Use computers for studying.

- 음료수, 껌, 캔디 등의 모든 음식물의 소지 및 반입이 금지됩니다.

  ⋙ Absolutely no food, drink, gum, or candy permitted.

- 수업 중 다른 학생들의 의견을 존중하며 남의 의견을 비난하지 않습니다.

  ⋙ Respect all ideas given in class and do not criticize anybody's ideas and thoughts.

- 늘 최선을 다합시다.

  ⋙ Do your very best all the time!

### 3) 식당 예절 (Cafeteria Etiquette)

- 12시 30분부터 1시 30분까지 점심시간입니다. 학생들은 질서정연하게 식당으로 들어가 주시기 바랍니다.

  ⋙ Lunch is from 12:30 to 1:30. Students should enter the cafeteria through the doors in an orderly manner.

급식 담당교사의 지도에 따라 줄을 섭니다. 새치기를 한 학생은 줄의 맨 끝으로 갑니다.

Students will be directed by the cafeteria supervisor to form a line. Students observed cutting ahead of others will be placed at the end of the line.

배식판을 들고 정해진 탁자로 가서 식사를 끝마칠 때까지 자리를 이동하지 않습니다.

Students should pick up their lunches and proceed to their eating area and should not move from one table to another after or during eating.

모든 음식물 쓰레기는 탁자나 바닥에 버려서는 안 되고 준비된 통에 버립니다.

All leftovers should never be left on the tables or floor. They should be thrown into the bucket.

음식물을 흘렸을 때는 급식 도우미의 도움을 받아 청소합니다.

If you spill something, you should get help from a cafeteria helper to clean it up.

음식물은 식당 밖으로 가지고 갈 수 없습니다.

No food is to be taken outside of the cafeteria at any time.

식사를 마친 후에는 식판을 퇴식구에 놓습니다.

As you finish eating, you are to take your tray and the dishes to the dishwashing area.

식사예절을 지킵시다.

Use good table manners at all times.

## 4) 공중위생과 건강 (Sanitation and Health Care)

체육시간 후엔 반드시 샤워를 하고 교실에 들어오기 바랍니다. 그리고 젖은 체육복은 빨아서 햇볕에 말리기 바랍니다. 젖은 채로 교실에 방치해서 냄새가 나지 않도록 하기 바랍니다.

After physical education, please take a shower and come to the class. Wash your sports gear and dry them in the sun. Never leave wet clothes in the classroom, because they will smell.

탈의실을 깨끗이 사용합시다. 옷을 바닥에 벗어 놓지 말고 옷걸이에 단정하게 걸어 놓기 바랍니다.

Please keep the locker room clean. Don't leave clothes on the floor but put them on the hangers.

식중독에 걸리기 쉬운 계절입니다. 항상 주변을 청결히 하고 비위생적으로 만들어진 음식물을 먹지 마십시오.

You can easily get food poisoning. Please keep your surroundings clean and don't eat food that has not been prepared hygienically.

오늘은 날이 몹시 습하고 덥습니다. 바깥출입을 자제하고 햇볕에 오랫동안 노출하지 않도록 하기 바랍니다. 일사병에 걸릴 위험이 있습니다.

Today is really sticky and hot. Please stay inside as much as possible and don't go out in the sun. You are likely to get sunstroke.

날이 덥다고 노출이 심한 옷을 입는 학생들이 늘고 있습니다. 깔끔한 복장을 해서 지내기 바랍니다. 그리고 수업 시간 중에 체육복을 입고 있지 않도록 합시다.

More and more students wear less and show more because it is hot. Dress neatly and cleanly. Please don't wear gym clothes during the class.

더운 날 많이 움직이면 쉬 피곤해집니다. 가능한 활동을 자제하고 충분한 휴식을 취하기 바랍니다.

If you are too active on a hot day, you will soon be tired. Please moderate your activity and get enough rest.

밀걸레를 깨끗하고 위생적으로 보관합시다. 더러운 밀걸레로 교실을 청소하면 더 불결해질 수도 있습니다. 그리고 청소 후 밀걸레는 깨끗한 상태로 말려 놓기 바랍니다.

Please keep the mops sanitary. If you use dirty mops, the classrooms will get dirtier. After cleaning up, dry the mops in the open air.

오늘은 날이 너무 더운 관계로 5분 단축 수업을 하겠습니다. 그래서 휴식 시간이 5분 길어지겠습니다.

As it is so hot today, we will shorten the class period by 5 minutes. So you will have a 5 minute longer break.

오늘 11시에 오존 경보가 내렸습니다. 경보가 해제될 때까지 가능한 밖에 나가지 않도록 하기 바랍니다. 피부가 오존에 오랫동안 노출되면 피부암에 걸릴 수도 있습니다.

There was an ozone warning at 11:00 a. m. Please don't go out until the warning is lifted. If your skin is exposed to ultraviolet light for too long, you might get skin cancer.

## 5) 재활용과 학교 환경보존 (Recycling and School Building and Grounds Maintenance)

화장실을 거실처럼 깨끗하고 청결하게 사용합시다.

Please, keep the rest rooms clean and sanitary.

쓰레기 양을 줄이도록 합시다. 그리고 분리수거를 실천해주기 바랍니다.

Please try to reduce the amount of waste. Practice separating the recyclables from other garbage.

각 반에서는 깡통, 플라스틱, 휴지 그리고 다른 쓰레기를 분리해서 수거할 수 있도록 별도의 쓰레기통을 비치하기 바랍니다.

Each class will be furnished with separate waste bins for the recyclables such as tin cans, plastic, papers and for other garbage.

주번 학생들은 쓰레기통을 제때 버려서 통이 넘치지 않도록 합시다. 그리고 항상 뚜껑을 덮어서 벌레들이 몰려들지 않도록 합시다.

Students on weekly duty are requested to empty waste bins before they become full. Remember to cover the waste bins to keep bugs out.

## 6) 에너지 절약 (Energy Conservation)

날이 무척 덥습니다. 11시부터 에어컨을 틀 예정이니 모든 문을 꼭 닫도록 하십시오. 실내온도와 실외온도 차이가 5도 정도 되게끔 온도를 조절하시길 바랍니다.

The weather is sweltering. Air conditioners will be turned on 11 a.m., so close all the doors and windows. Please adjust the air conditioners to keep the temperature in the classroom at 5 degrees lower than that outside.

특별실로 이동시에는 전등과 에어컨을 끄고 이동하기 바랍니다. 그리고 문단속도 확실히 하기 바랍니다.

When you go to special classrooms, please turn off the lights and the air conditioner in your homeroom. Please lock your classroom when you leave.

주번들은 하교할 시 교실 선풍기가 모두 꺼졌는지 확인하기 바랍니다. 밤새 선풍기가 켜져 있으면 과열이 되어 화재가 발생할 수 있으니 특히 유념하기 바랍니다.

>>> The students on weekly duty are required to make sure that all the fans are off when you go home. Please remember that when the fans are left on overnight they can overheat and catch fire.

가뭄이 심합니다. 모두 물을 아껴 쓰도록 합시다. 가정에서도 허드렛물로 화초에 물을 주고 수돗물을 잠궈서 물을 낭비하는 일이 없도록 합시다.

>>> We have a serious drought. Let's save water. At home, water plants or flowers with recycled water and turn off the tap so as not to waste water.

이번 주는 '자연 보호 주간'입니다. 자연 보호에 적극 동참하여 아름다운 환경을 후손들에게 물려줄 수 있도록 합시다.

>>> This week is 'Nature Preservation Week.' Please take an active part in preserving nature, so we can pass on this beautiful environment to our descendants.

다음 주 금요일에는 학교 주변 청소 및 청소년 유해 업소 출입 금지 운동을 벌이겠습니다.

>>> Next Friday, we will clean up the areas around the school and carry out a campaign to stop juveniles from entering facilities prohibited to minors.

교내 및 주변 청소를 실시하겠습니다. 학생들은 쓰레기 봉투를 가져가시고 재활용품을 분리하여 주십시오. 본관 앞에서 모여주십시오. 그리고 각반 선생님께서는 청소구역을 확인하시기 바랍니다.

>>> Cleaning up the school campus and the surrounding areas will begin soon. Please take plastic bags with you. Also, please separate the recyclables. Meet in front of the main building. The teachers are asked to make sure

they know where the cleaning area is.

### 7) 대중교통 이용하기 (Using Public Transportation)

자가용을 타고 등교하지 말고 대중교통 수단을 이용하기 바라며, 학교 앞까지 자가용을 타고 등교하는 일이 없도록 합시다.

>>> Please use public transportation instead of coming to school by car, and don't get out of your car only just in front of the school.

## 6. 기타 (Others)

수업시간 변경, 급식, 학생회 간부 선출, 재난 방지 훈련과 체력검사와 헌혈을 안내할 때 쓸 수 있는 표현이다.

### 1) 수업 시간 안내 (Bell Schedule)

2교시 수업은 10분 늦게 시작하겠습니다. 하지만 종전과 같이 11시에 수업을 마치겠습니다.

>>> The second period will start ten minutes late. But it will end at 11 as

usual.

첫 주는 임시 시간표대로 수업을 운영하겠습니다. 다음 주에 새로운 시간표를 발표할 예정입니다.

≫ This first week, classes will be held according to the temporary schedule. Next week, a new time table will be announced.

종이 잘못 울렸습니다. 정상적으로 2시부터 5교시가 시작됩니다. 착오 없으시기 바랍니다.

≫ I'm sorry, but it was the wrong bell. The fifth class will start at 2 as normal. Don't be confused, please.

정전이 되어 시보가 작동이 안 됩니다. 선생님들은 시계를 보시고 수업에 임하시기 바랍니다.

≫ As the power is off, the bell doesn't work. The teachers are asked to go by their watches.

이번주 특별활동 시간에는 학급 임원들을 선출하도록 하겠습니다. 학생들은 누구를 임원으로 선출할지 생각해 두시고 적극 투표에 임하기 바랍니다.

≫ This week, during the club activity class, you will have an election for the class council. Consider carefully who should be your representatives and vote for your choice.

5분 생활영어 시간입니다. 모두 방송에 귀 기울여 주시기 바랍니다.

»» This is the time for 5-minute everyday English. Please listen to the intercom.

오늘 배운 표현들을 교과서에 적어 두십시오. 하루에 한 가지 표현을 꾸준히 배우면 일 년 동안 많은 표현을 배우게 될 겁니다.

»» Please write down today's expression in your book. If you learn one expression a day, you will have learned a lot of expressions over a year.

아침 7시 10분부터 방송 수업이 시작되겠습니다. 교실의 모니터를 켜고 수업 준비를 하기 바랍니다. 수업 시간 중에 조는 학생이 없도록 합시다.

»» The distance learning program will start at 7:10. Please turn on the monitors and be ready for the class. Please stay awake during the class. No nodding off.

'나의 주장' 발표 시간입니다. 오늘은 1학년 1반 김희원양이 '지구 온난화'에 대해 주장을 발표하겠습니다. 발표 시간은 5분입니다. 잘 듣고 여러분은 '지구 온난화'에 대한 여러분의 생각을 돌아보는 시간이 되길 바랍니다.

»» Now is the time for presenting 'My Opinion'. Today, Miss. Kim, Heui-Won from Class 1 of the first grade will speak for 5 minutes on 'Global Warming.' Listen to what Miss. Kim says and think about what your responses will be.

### 2) 급식 (School Lunch)

4교시를 마친 후, 급식 당번들은 식당으로 내려오십시오. 음식을 운반할 때

데지 않도록 특히 유의하기 바랍니다.

⋙ After fourth period, the students in charge of distributing food should come down to the cafeteria. When you carry the food, take extra care so as not to get burned.

학교 급식 식단은 매달 초에 게시판에 공고하겠습니다. 그리고 조만간 급식에 대한 여러분의 의견을 물어보는 조사를 실시하고자 합니다.

⋙ School lunch menus will be posted on the bulletin board at the beginning of each month. There will be a survey regarding the school lunch menus.

이번 달은 3학년이 먼저 식사를 하고 다음 달은 2학년이 먼저 식사를 하도록 하겠습니다. 식당에서는 줄을 서서 조용히 기다리기 바랍니다.

⋙ This month, the third grade students will have lunch first and next month, the second grade students. In the cafeteria, please line up quietly.

식사를 마친 후 식탁 밑으로 의자를 밀어 넣고 자리를 뜨기 바랍니다. 그리고 잔반을 남기지 않도록 적당량을 떠가기 바랍니다. 음식에 대해 욕심을 내지 않도록 합시다.

⋙ After lunch, put the chairs back under the table before you leave. Please don't take more food than you can eat and leave no leftovers. Make sure that your eyes are not bigger than your stomach!

### 3) 학생회 간부선출 (Election for Student's Council Staff)

신학기 학생회 간부를 선출하고자 합니다. 선거에 입후보하고자 하는 학생은 이 달 20일까지 등록을 마쳐주십시오.

≫ There will be an election for Students' Council. Those who want to run for the election should register no later than the 20th of this month.

학생회 회장과 부회장에 출마한 학생들에게는 오늘부터 1주일간의 공식 선거운동 기간이 주어집니다. 이번 선거가 공정하게 이루어지는 것이 매우 중요합니다.

≫ The students who are going to run for the Students' Council president and vice president will be given a week-long official campaign period, which will start today. It is very important for this election to be fair and just.

오늘은 학생회 간부 선출을 위한 선거가 있는 날입니다. 적극적으로 선거에 참가합시다.

≫ Today is election day for selecting the Students' Council. Please take an active part in the election.

이번 선거는 직접 선거로 행해지며 여러분들의 한 표 한 표가 소중합니다. 누가 우리를 가장 잘 대변해줄 사람인가를 신중히 생각한 후에 투표에 임하기 바랍니다.

≫ The result of this election will be determined by individual votes, so each of your votes will count. Please think carefully about who will be your best representatives, and vote accordingly.

투표장은 체육관에 설치되어 있습니다. 투표는 1학년 1반, 1학년 2반 등의 순서로 시작하겠습니다.

The election will be held in the gym. Class 1-1 will vote first and then Class 1-2 and so on, in that order.

무효표가 없도록 투표시 주의 사항을 잘 숙지하고 투표에 임하기 바랍니다.

Please make sure you know all the procedures for casting a vote, so that there will be no invalid votes.

선거 결과를 말씀드리겠습니다. 김현빈이 300표로 260표를 얻은 박인호군을 누르고 학생회 대표로 선출되었습니다.

Here is the result of the election. Mr. Kim Hyun-Bin received 300 votes, while Mr. Pack In-ho received 260. Therefore, Mr. Kim Hyun-Bin is the new president of the Students' Council.

김현빈군의 당선 소감을 들어보겠습니다.

Mr. Kim Hyun-Bin will deliver his acceptance speech.

### 4) 재난방지 훈련 (Disaster Drill)

오늘은 재난방지 훈련의 날입니다. 사이렌이 울리면 신속히 교실에서 비상 계단을 따라 한 줄로 밖으로 나오길 바랍니다. 훈련은 2시부터 2시 20분까지 20분간 실시되겠습니다.

>>> Today there is a disaster drill. Please leave the classroom immediately when you hear the siren and walk down the emergency stairs in a single row. The drill will take place for 20 minutes at 2 p.m. and finish at 2:20.

오늘 오후 2시부터 한 시간 동안 소방 훈련을 실시하겠습니다. 오늘 상황은 2층 중앙현관에서 화재가 발생하여 건물 전체로 번진 것입니다. 사이렌이 울리면 교실에서 즉시 대피하여 축구장으로 모여 주십시오. 침착하게 입을 막고 줄을 서서 비상계단을 이용하십시오.

>>> Today there is a fire drill from 2 p.m. lasting for an hour. Today's scenario is that a fire starts in the middle of the second floor and it spreads to the entire building. Please evacuate the classroom immediately, and gather on the soccer field when you hear the siren. Please stay clam and use the emergency stairs in a row with your mouth covered.

운동장에서는 119 소방관들이 소화기로 불을 끄는 법에 대해 시범을 보여주시겠습니다. 시범 후에는 학생여러분이 직접 소화기를 사용하는 방법을 연습하겠습니다.

>>> The fire fighters from the 119 center will demonstrate how to extinguish a fire with an extinguisher. After the demonstration, students will practice how to use an extinguisher.

오늘의 지진 대피훈련은 오후 2시부터 40분간 실시됩니다. 오늘 훈련 상황은 15일 8시 55분경 충남 홍성에서 강한 지진이 발생하여 전기와 가스, 수도관을 포함한 대부분의 중요한 도시 기반시설이 파괴되는 상황입니다. 오늘 훈련의 목적은 땅이 흔들리는 조짐이 있을 때 즉각적으로 적절하게 대처하는 법을 학생들이 배울 수 있도록 돕는 것입니다. 학생들은 어디로 대피해야 하는지, 어떻게 자신들을 보호하는지를 알아야 할 것입니다.

≫ Today's earthquake drill starts at 2 p.m. and lasts for 40 minutes in the afternoon. The drill scenario started out with a strong earthquake hitting Hongsung, Chungnam Province around 8:55 a.m., destroying much of the city's critical infrastructure, including power, gas and water lines. The purpose is to help students learn how to react immediately and appropriately at the first indication of ground shaking. Students should know where to seek shelter, and how to protect themselves.

지진 대피 행동은 다음과 같습니다. 먼저 교실에 있는 학생들은 건물 밖으로 나가지 말고 엎드려 몸을 숨긴 채 지진이 끝날 때 까지 기다리십시오. 창가나 문 쪽은 피하도록 합니다. 운동장에 있는 학생들은 건물, 나무, 전선과 멀리 떨어진 곳으로 피하여 지진이 끝날 때 까지 땅에 엎드려 있기 바랍니다.

≫ Earthquake drills are as follows. For students indoors, stay inside and drop, cover, and hold on. Stay away from windows and doors. For students outdoors, find a clear spot away from buildings, trees, and power lines and drop to the ground until the shaking stops.

## 5) 체력검사와 헌혈 (Physical Fitness Assessment and Blood Donation)

체력검사를 실시하겠습니다. 학생들은 체육복으로 갈아입고 운동장에 모이기 바랍니다.

>>> Physical fitness assessment will take place soon. Please come out to the field in sports gear.

실장은 나누어준 유인물에 있는 검사 순서대로 학생들을 이동시키기 바랍니다. 검사 종목은 50미터 달리기, 윗몸 일으키기, 턱걸이, 매달리기, 멀리뛰기, 1000미터 달리기, 800미터 달리기입니다. 장거리 달리기는 점심 식사 후에 하겠습니다.

>>> Class presidents are asked to confirm the order of the assessments in the handouts and lead your classes accordingly. The assessments are on the 50-meter run, sit-ups, chin-ups, pull-ups, standing jump, 1000-meter run, and 800-meter run. Distance running events will take place after lunch.

헌혈을 하고자 하는 학생들은 지금 운동장에 있는 적십자 혈액원에서 나온 차량으로 가기 바랍니다. 여러분의 헌혈이 많은 사람들의 생명을 구할 수 있다는 사실을 명심하고 많이 참여할 수 있도록 합시다.

>>> Students who want to give blood are asked to go to the Red Cross vehicle in the playground. Your blood donation can save many people's lives, so please join the blood giving drive.

# 부 록

## 1. 식당 메뉴 (Cafeteria Menu)

### 밥 종류__Rice dishes

콩나물밥___bean sprouts over rice

떡볶이___spicy rice cake (strings)

(김치) 볶음밥___(Kimchi) fried rice

비빔밥___rice mixed with meat, seasoned vegetables and egg

김밥___Korean roll

고구마 맛탕___deep-fried sugar glazed sweet potatoes

자장밥___rice topped with black soy bean sauce

김치 제육덮밥__rice topped with stir-fried kimchi and pork

낙지덮밥__rice topped with stir-fried baby octopus

영양밥__boiled rice with various nutritious ingredients

야채비빔밥__vegetable *bibimbap*

보리밥__Steamed Rice w/Barley corn

### 죽 종류__Porridge dishes

닭죽___chicken porridge

잣죽___pine nut porridge

호박죽___pumpkin porridge

야채죽___vegetable porridge

전복죽___rice porridge with abalone

영양죽___chestnut and rice porridge

## 국수 종류__Noodle dishes

콩국수__bean noodles

자장면__Chinese style noodles

잡채__glass noodle stir fry

소바, 모밀국수__Japanese style buckwheat noodles

장국수__market noodles

냉면__cold buckwheat noodles

쫄면__chewy cold noodles

## 반찬__Side dishes

멸치 볶음__anchovy stir fry

양념두부__boiled tofu with seasoning

파전, 부추전__scallion pancake

단호박전__pan-fried sweet pumpkin

김치전__kimchi pancake

계란말이__folded egg

군만두__fried dumplings

김치만두__dumplings stuffed with kimchi

녹두묵__Mung bean cake

마늘 장아찌__pickled garlic

감자부침__pan fried potato cake

(양념한)도토리묵__seasoned acorn jelly

콩나물 무침__seasoned bean sprouts

시금치 무침__seasoned spinach

가지나물__seasoned Eggplant

계란찜__steamed egg

계란탕__egg soup

두부(양념)튀김__fried tofu cake

배추김치___cabbage kimchi
무김치___radish kimchi
김치참치찌게___kimchi tuna soup
김치두부 전___fried kimchi and tofu cake
김치부침___kimchi stir fry
고등어조림___braised mackerel
두부김치___tofu kimchi
골뱅이무침___spicy freshwater snails
해파리냉채___jellyfish cold plate
해물냉채___seafood cold plate
깍두기___diced radish kimchi
낙지볶음___stir-fried baby octopus
미역초무침___seaweed and cucumber salad
도토리묵___acorn starch jelly
미역냉국___chilled seaweed soup
순두부___soft tofu
오징어초무침___boiled squid with vinegared red pepper paste
생선가스___fish cutlet
양념통닭___roast chicken coated with sweet, tangy sauce
닭갈비___pan-fried chicken ribs
닭강정___deep-fried and glazed chicken
돼지갈비___grilled pork ribs
탕수육___sweet and sour pork(beef)

### 국__Soup

미역국___seaweed soup
된장국___soybean paste soup
삼계탕___chicken ginseng soup
곰탕___boiled bone stew with rice

떡국___Sliced rice pasta soup

떡만두국___Sliced rice pasta soup with dumplings

만둣국___dumpling soup

해물탕___Seafood stew

## 2. 식당에서의 주요 표현 (Cafeteria Expressions)

- Did you all wash your hands? (모두 손을 씻었나요?)
- Stand in a line, please. (한 줄로 서세요.)
- The second graders are first. (2학년이 우선입니다.)
- Do not cut in the line. (새치기 하지 마세요.)
- Practice today's expression while you're waiting.
  (기다리는 동안 오늘의 표현을 연습하세요.)
- Be quiet, please. (조용히 하세요.)
- Have a seat here. (여기에 앉으세요.)
- Do not leave your food. (음식을 남기지 마세요.)
- Pass me that, please. (그것을 건네주세요.)
- Put leftovers here. (잔반을 여기에 버리세요.)
- The exit is over there. (출구는 저기입니다.)
- It's too salty / sour / sweet / bitter / bland.
  (너무 짜다 / 시다 / 달다 / 쓰다 / 담백하다.)
- It smells great. (냄새가 좋다.)
- It looks yummy. (맛있게 보인다.)
- It looks delicious. (맛있게 보인다.)
- It tastes very good. (맛이 매우 좋다.)
- Let's eat before it gets cold. (식기 전에 먹자.)

- Chew well. (꼭꼭 씹으세요.)
- Don't chew noisily. (소리 내서 씹지 마세요.)
- Let's take some food in a small bowl. (작은 그릇에 음식을 담읍시다.)
- Don't talk with your mouth full. (입에 음식이 있을 때는 말하지 마세요.)
- Take a spoonful of rice. (한 숟가락 가득 밥을 뜨세요.)
- Don't spill food. (음식을 흘리지 마세요.)
- It tastes different. (맛이 다른데요.)
- Don't eat so much. (너무 많이 먹지 마세요.)
- Don't overeat. (과식하지 마세요.)
- Don't pig out like that. (그렇게 많이 먹지 마세요.)
- Slow down. (천천히.)
- You will get indigestion. (너 체할거야.)
- Be careful, it's hot. (뜨거우니 조심해요.)
- How does it taste? (맛이 어때요?)
- That was a wonderful meal. (훌륭한 식사였어요.)
- Don't be picky about food. (골고루 먹으세요.)
- Have some more. (더 드세요.)
- Give this a try. (이것을 먹어 보세요.)
- Do you want more? (더 먹을래요?)
- Are you full? (배가 부르니?)
- No thanks. I'm already full. (I've had enough.) (괜찮습니다. 배불러요.)
- Finish the food on your dish. (접시에 있는 음식을 모두 먹으세요.)
- Did you have enough? (많이 먹었어요?)
- Let's clean up the table. (식탁을 치웁시다.)
- Go ahead. Help yourself. (어서 많이 먹어요.)

# 참고문헌


김인옥 & L. Rowley. (2007). 활동으로 익히는 교실영어. 서울: 형설출판사.

박경수. (2000). 영어교육론. 서울: 형설 출판사.

박 원. (1993). 학교 생활 영어 School Life in English Ⅲ. 서울: 범영출판사.

부산광역시교육과학연구원. (2001) 인터넷으로 만나는 신나는 영어수업. 부산인쇄 정보산업협동조합.

부산광역시 교육청. (2000). 영어로 진행하는 영어 수업 모범 교수·학습지도안. 부산 인쇄공업협동조합.

서미석. (2007). 미국초등학교에서 쓰는 왁자지껄 교실영어. 서울: 넥서스.

임병빈, 연준흠, 장경숙. (1998). 영어교사 연수와 현장연구 방법. 서울: 신아사.

정동빈 외. (1997). 어린이 영어교육. 서울: 홍익미디어.

정동빈 외. (2000). Classroom English. 서울: 학문출판사.

정창복 역. (1998). 과학자를 위한 영어 구두발표 방법. 서울: 월드사이언스.

조일제. (2005). 교실영어와 수업모형. 서울: 우용출판사.

조일제 역. (1997). 영어교사를 위한 영문학 작품 지도법. 서울: 한국문화사.

주간 일요시사. 2001. 7. 7. 어린이 영어교육 열풍: 외국인 교사와 24시간 영어로 생활하기.

한국관광공사. (2005). 외국어 관광안내 표기 용례집.

한국교육과정 평가원. (2000). 교실영어(Classroom English).

홍진옥. (1999). 21세기를 위한 초등영어지도. 서울: 민지사.

황기동. (2004). 누구나 영어로 가르칠 수 있다. 서울: 어문학사.

황기동 외. (1998). 교실 영어의 이해와 실제. 서울: 서울외국서적.

Arnold, E. (1987). English Alive: Dramatized Conversation Course Book Ⅰ. Seoul: CPI.

Arnold, E. (1987). English Alive: Dramatized Conversation Course Book Ⅱ. Seoul: CPI.

Ely, C. & 조숙희 (2005). 영어 선생님을 위한 서바이벌 교실영어. 서울: 범문사.

Fitzpatrick, A. (1987). A English for International Conferences. Seoul: CPI.

Hughes, G. S. (1981). A Handbook of Classroom English. Oxford: Oxford University Press.

Greenwood, J. (1997). Activity Box. Cambridge: Cambridge University Press.

Keller, E. & S. T. Warner. (1990) Conversation Gambits. Hove: Language Teaching Publications.

Porter, P. A. & G. Margaret. (1992). Communicating Effectively in English. Belmont, California: Wardsworth.

Walker, M. (1992). Addison-Wesley ESL. New York: Addison-Wesley Publishing.

Willis, Jane. (1981). Teaching English through English. Essex: Longman Group Ltd.

Wright, A. (1989). Pictures for Language Learning. Cambridge: Cambridge University Press.

저자


**엄철주**

전남대학교 인문대학 영어영문학과 졸업
미국 University of Texas at Austin 응용언어학 박사
현) 전남대학교 사범대학 영어교육과 교수

**오경옥**

전남대학교 인문대학 영어영문학과 졸업
전남대학교 대학원 영어교육학 박사과정 수료
현) 광주 문흥중학교 교사

**오희진**

전남대학교 사범대학 영어교육과 졸업
전남대학교 대학원 영어교육학 박사과정 수료
현) 전남외국어고등학교 교사

**김희화**

전남대학교 인문대학 영어영문학과 졸업
현) 광주 유덕중학교 교사


교사들을 위한

**교실영어와 학교영어**


인쇄 | 2008년 12월 25일
발행 | 2008년 12월 30일

저자 | 엄철주 · 오경옥 · 오희진 · 김희화
발행 | 김윤수
발행처 | 전남대학교출판부

등록 | 1981. 5. 21. 제53호
주소 | 500-757 광주광역시 북구 용봉로 77
전화 | (062) 530-0571~3
팩스 | (062) 530-0579
홈페이지 | http://altair.chonnam.ac.kr/~cnup

값 10,000원

ISBN 978-89-7598-702-1 (13740)

이 도서의 국립중앙도서관 출판시도서목록(CIP)은 e-CIP홈페이지 (http://www.nl.go.kr/ecip)에서 이용하실 수 있습니다.
(CIP제어번호: CIP2008003878)